ANDREW FLINTOFF
THE BIOGRAPHY

ANDREW FLINTOFF
THE BIOGRAPHY

TIM EWBANK

JB
JOHN BLAKE

Published by John Blake Publishing Ltd,
3 Bramber Court, 2 Bramber Road,
London W14 9PB, England

www.blake.co.uk

First published in hardback in 2006

ISBN 978 1 84454 525 4

British Library Cataloguing-in-Publication Data:

A catalogue record for this book is available from the British Library.

Design by www.envydesign.co.uk

Printed in the UK by CPI Bookmarque, Croydon, CR0 4TD

1 3 5 7 9 10 8 6 4 2

Papers used by John Blake Publishing are natural, recyclable products made from wood grown in sustainable forests. The manufacturing processes conform to the environmental regulations of the country of origin.

Pictures reproduced by kind permission of A.P., Cleva, Empics, Getty Images, Mirrorpix

DEDICATION

For my father, Henry Ewbank, and my grandfather Tim Barrett, passionate cricket lovers both, who together first introduced me to the wonders of the game. And to my mother Joy who, with my father, paved the way for me to live the dream of playing cricket at Lord's by sending me to Tonbridge School.

Acknowledgements

For their assistance, enthusiasm and encouragement, the author would like to thank David Aers, John Airey, Richard Allibone, Bill Barr, David Bowditch, Russell Bradley, Dwayne Bravo, David Brooks, John Burmester, Paul Burnham and the Barmy Army, Mike Bushby, Philip Caldwell, Peter Canney, Nick Clough, Michael de St. Croix, Corinna and Chris Cowie, Roger Davis, Ray Dovey, Robin Eggar, Dr David English, John Etheridge, William Eve, Carole Anne Ferris, Peter Flower, John Forester-Walker, William Franklyn, Rod and Joy Gilchrist, Richard Gracey, Arthur Hull, Chris Hull, Clive Jackson, Jerry Johns, David Kemp, Barry Kernon, Alan Kingston, Fiona Knight, Roger Knight, John Knott, Lancashire County Cricket Club, Frank Langan, John Lloyd, Aidan MacEchern, Moira Marr, MCC,

Kit Miller, Philip Mitchell, Tony Monteuuis, Peter Morris, Roger Morris, Mike Page, Yvonne and Richard Partridge, Peter and Helen Pasea, James Pitt, Roger Poulet, Peter Prendergast, David Reeve, Tony Rice-Oxley, Keith Richmond, Alasdair Riley, Ian Robertson, Jeff Rooke, St Anne's Cricket Club, Sky Sports, Martin Smith, George Still, Steve Stowell, TalkSport radio, Hugh Tebay, Charles Tilling, Graham Tindall, Fred Titmus, David Toft, Robbie Ward, Cynthia Warrington, Ferris Whidborne, Ros White, Mike Young.

In a book containing many statistics, every effort has been made to ensure accuracy, and the author would like to acknowledge *Wisden Cricketers' Almanack* as an invaluable source of data. Other important sources include: the *Sun*, the *Mirror*, *The Times*, *Observer Sport Monthly*, the *Daily Telegraph*, the *Guardian*, the *Independent*, the *Lancashire Evening Post*, the *Daily Mail*, the *Daily Express*, the *News Of The World*. The author is also indebted to Channel 4 and Sky Sports for their excellent TV coverage of Andrew Flintoff's exploits for England.

Special thanks to Stafford Hildred for his collaboration, to Chew Magna's much valued all-rounder, Simon Kinnersley, for his input and his enthusiastic company at every Test Match at Lord's over the past twenty-five years, and to Oliver and Emma Ewbank for their patience during the writing of this book.

Finally, my gratitude goes to publisher John Blake and editor Michelle Signore.

Contents

Introduction

Anyone who has followed Andrew Flintoff's international cricket career has known all along that he had it in him to become a truly exceptional all-rounder. From the moment he was capped by England at the age of twenty, we believed he had the talent, the ability and the phenomenal power in his 6ft 4in frame to become one of the most exciting and hard-hitting batsmen in world cricket.

But injury, loss of form and a lack of understanding on his part of what was required to succeed at the highest level delayed his rise to the position he now occupies as a national hero, an outstanding all-rounder who plays the game with infectious enthusiasm and with a spirit of adventure that has made him England's best-loved cricketer since Ian Botham.

For England fans, and for Flintoff himself, it was a

frustrating wait for him to do himself full justice. Then, on a sun-kissed Sunday at Lord's in August 2003, all of us who had championed Andrew Flintoff for so long could finally turn around and say, 'I told you so.' On that day he made a blistering 142 against South Africa, and – injuries notwithstanding – he has barely looked back.

Until then, we followers of Flintoff's fortunes had watched nervously as he all too frequently misfired and underachieved. We endured with him those reckless too-early dismissals when he tried injudiciously to slog the ball into next week, those moments when crafty Test spinners bamboozled him and made him look inept, even foolish. But suddenly, on that glorious Lord's Sunday, all was forgiven as Flintoff stood tall when those around him had failed. Thrillingly, at the headquarters of cricket, he proceeded to put the South African attack to the sword. And how we all rose to our feet and cheered.

The origin for the idea for this book was that sensational innings, which I was lucky enough to see. And I know exactly where I was sitting at Lord's in the summer of 2004 when he smote seven exhilarating sixes in an unforgettable innings of 123 against the West Indies.

I was also lucky enough, and privileged, to get to every England–Australia Test match in the summer of 2005. I will never forget the excitement and the drama of the greatest series of them all, nor Flintoff's monumental contribution to England winning back the Ashes.

INTRODUCTION

The cricket world universally knows Andrew Flintoff as 'Freddie', after the cartoon character Fred Flintstone, and in the writing of this book it seemed appropriate to call him by the name by which he is most popularly known.

Inevitably, in a biography about a young man who has spent most of his adult life on the cricket field, this book contains many statistics, and every effort has been made to ensure their accuracy and that mistakes are kept to a minimum.

Finally, I would like to thank my father, Henry, and my grandfather, Tim, for introducing me to the wonders of cricket. I like to think that they would have enjoyed this book.

CHAPTER 1

A Born Cricketer

> 'I played my first game, for the Under-Fourteens, when I was six. My brother, Chris, was the captain then, and I was sent off to field on the boundary. I remember I played in my tracksuit bottoms as I didn't have any proper kit, and I scored one, not out. It was from that moment that I fell in love with cricket.'
>
> ANDREW FLINTOFF

It had been a memorable few months for British sport when Andrew Flintoff came into the world in Preston, Lancashire, towards the end of 1977. Earlier that year, on her sixteenth attempt, Virginia Wade had at last won the Ladies' Singles tennis title in Wimbledon's Championship Centenary Year, and she had done it in front of the Queen, who had been paying a rare visit to Wimbledon in her Silver Jubilee year; Red Rum – one of the best-loved horses ever to run at Aintree – had galloped away to his record third Grand National victory; and England had wrested back the Ashes with a convincing three–nil home series win in the centenary year of England–Australia Tests. In the general euphoria of victory, special mention was being made about an exciting new all-rounder England had unearthed by the name of Ian

Botham. The Somerset all-rounder had burst on to the scene with bat and ball and played no small part in England's cricketers winning back the precious urn.

On Tuesday, 6 December 1977, the day that Freddie made his entrance into the world, England's cricketers were on tour in Pakistan, enjoying a rest day in between two not-out centuries scored by Geoff Boycott in Faisalabad, first against the United Bank XI and then against the Northwestern Frontier Governor's XI.

This was the same Geoff Boycott of Yorkshire who that summer of 1977 had hit his 100th First-Class 100 with a Test century for England against the Australians on his home ground at Headingley and who, years later, would admiringly watch Freddie in powerful six-hitting mode and, in his role as TV pundit, exclaim to millions of viewers, 'Exciting, isn't it? I wish I could bat like that!'

Freddie was born into a Britain where Labour's Jim Callaghan was Prime Minister, inflation had just dropped to 11 per cent, the average house price in London and the Southeast was £16,731 and *Saturday Night Fever* – the film that turned disco into a multi-million-dollar industry – was about to be released and make John Travolta the hottest young star in showbusiness.

Freddie's home town of Preston, situated some forty miles north of Manchester, was originally a Lancashire market town, built on the River Ribble, which developed into a centre of the textiles industry and then into an engineering centre, incorporating large industrial plants. Before the recent Flintoff exploits on the cricket field, if you mentioned 'Preston' and 'sport' in the same breath, most people would associate the town with Preston North End, one of the oldest of football clubs. And that club is forever associated with its legendary star player Tom (now Sir Tom) Finney.

The pride of Preston, Finney was considered by many to have been the most complete British footballer of all time and, even in a golden age of soccer in the 1940s and 1950s, he was outstanding. He won seventy-six caps for England and was once his country's leading goal-scorer, in one year putting away a total of thirty. 'Tom Finney would have been great in any team, in any match, in any age, even if he'd been wearing an overcoat,' said the great Liverpool manager Bill Shankly.

Swedish group ABBA's 'The Name Of The Game' was at the top of the British charts when Freddie was born but, in Colin and Susan Flintoff's semi-detached house in Preston, there was no doubting that the name of the game was not football but cricket. Freddie's father, Colin, who worked in maintenance for British Aerospace, was an ardent cricket fan and no mean club cricketer himself, while Freddie's mother, Susan, was a willing helper when it came to the team teas. Colin still regularly turns out for the 100-year-old village cricket club Whittingham and Goosnargh, which plays in Lancashire's Moore and Smalley Palace Shield League.

The Flintoffs already had a three-year-old boy, Christopher, when Freddie was born in 1977, and their second son's arrival occurred at a time when Colin and other supporters of Lancashire County Cricket Club didn't have much to celebrate. For the first time in sixty-seven years, an England squad bound for Australia contained not a single Lancashire player, a statistic that had followers of Lancashire cricket moaning that things certainly weren't what they used to be – especially as, in that year, the county team also endured their worst-ever season.

Lancashire seemingly had a pretty strong line-up, including the outstanding West Indian star Clive Lloyd and Preston's Frank Hayes, a batsman of special ability who became the toast of the town by scoring a century in his first Test match for England at Lord's. But Lancashire won only two of twenty-two County Championship matches that year, and their poor season ended with David Lloyd – who later would be so influential in Freddie's development at youth, county and international levels – tendering his resignation as Lancashire's captain after a five-year tenure.

Freddie also happened to be born at a time when the game his father loved was in utter turmoil at the highest level. The very structure of international cricket was being shaken to its long-standing and, until then, seemingly rock-solid foundations. For weeks, cricket was rarely off the front pages of newspapers while a bitter battle was waged for control of the world's leading players.

In May 1977, Australian publishing and media magnate Kerry Packer had shocked the Establishment by signing up thirty-five of the world's best cricketers on lucrative contracts for a series of specially arranged international matches to be played in the autumn. He was willing, he said, to plunge a staggering $9 million into putting his World Series Cricket – as he named it – on the map.

Later dubbed 'Packer's circus', the startling new World Series venture was seen by the game's administrators as a direct threat to official Test cricket and to the First-Class game, and it inevitably led to a deep rift between the world's leading cricketers and the officials who presided over the game. The International Cricket Conference's reaction to Packer's plans was to threaten to ban from Test cricket – and, by implication, from the entire First-Class game – all those players who did not revoke the contracts they had signed with Packer.

Just twelve days before Freddie's birth, Kerry Packer and his contracted players won their court action against the cricket authorities who were seeking to ban them from First-Class cricket because of their involvement in the cricket circus in Australia. On 25 November Mr Justice Slade ruled in London's High Court that a proposed ban on players who took part in the Australia v Overseas XI series was illegal, as it represented an unreasonable restraint of trade and an inducement for players to break their contracts with Packer.

The verdict represented a clear victory for Packer and for the three players – England's Tony Grieg and John Snow and South African Mike Procter – who had jointly sued the authorities. At the time, the cricket authorities might have been aghast at the way in which the game had apparently been hijacked from under their noses at the very highest level, but the Packer circus revolutionised cricket's One-Day game, not least by its introduction of coloured clothing for the players (initially sneered at by the staunch traditionalists as the attire of 'pyjama cricket').

Cricket had generally been undersold for many years, and Packer referred to it as the easiest sport in the world to take over. Why? Because nobody had bothered to pay the players what they were worth, he said. He put his money where his mouth was by paying out $100,000 in prize money to the world's elite cricketers for his series of matches. It was the start of a pay revolution that now sees the cream of the world's players, such as Andrew Flintoff, able to earn – with the help of central contracts, lucrative sponsorship deals and endorsements – something approaching £1 million a year. Packer's new, jazzed-up brand of brazenly commercial cricket, played in a carnival atmosphere and screened on TV to a wide audience on Channel 9 in Australia, attracted an inquisitive new kind of fan to the game as well as the die-hards. Packer also vigorously promoted the exciting, fast-action aspects of One-Day Internationals, which today attract sell-out crowds and encourage the kind of thrilling big-hitting that Freddie would bring to the England One-Day team a quarter of a century later.

As the son of a cricket fanatic, it was only natural that

Freddie's introduction to the game would come through his dad. Colin enjoyed playing cricket regularly at weekends, and Freddie – his hair a mass of blond curls – and his brother, Chris, became a familiar sight, looking on or playing with a bat and ball beyond the boundary line as they grew up. 'My own first cricketing memories are of watching my father playing cricket for Dutton Forshaw, near Preston,' recalls Freddie. 'He was the Second XI captain and my brother, Chris, played for the same team.

'I played my first game, for the Under-Fourteens, when I was six. Chris was the captain then, and I was sent off to field on the boundary. I remember I played in my tracksuit bottoms as I didn't have any proper kit, and I scored one, not out.'

Freddie was roped into playing that first game only because Chris's team were suddenly found to be a man short. He hadn't expected to play, which partly explains why he wasn't in whites but wearing a Manchester United tracksuit. Despite such a peripheral involvement in his very first game, however, Freddie was hooked. 'It was from that moment that I fell in love with cricket.'

From day one, however, Freddie learned that cricket can be a hard game and a great leveller. He might have done his best to keep his wicket intact for a solitary run and patrolled the boundary with enthusiasm in glaringly conspicuous non-cricket kit, but it wasn't enough for him to retain his place in the Under-Fourteens. 'The following week, I was dropped to the Under-Thirteens,' he recalls with a laugh, 'but, by the time I was eight, I was playing for Lancashire Under-Elevens.'

At Freddie's school, Greenlands County Primary, situated on a nearby council estate a short walk away from the family home, cricket – if played at all – was just a bit of knockabout fun in the break between lessons. Football was what all the other boys and his friends really enjoyed playing, and Freddie went along with it. It was clear, however, that he was a natural at all ball games, and table tennis was just one that came easily enough for him to go on to play for the local Deepdale team.

Being tall for his age as a schoolboy, Freddie also played mini-rugby. He remained skinny as he grew up, but it always looked as though the lanky boy was destined to end up a big, tall lad. He naturally filled out into his big frame by the time he had finished growing, and he later attracted the attention of the local rugby-union club Preston Grasshoppers, who knew all too well the value of having a player of exceptional height; one of their star players at the time was England's second-row giant Wade Dooley, who was affectionately known in the game as 'the Blackpool Tower' because of his mighty stature. At his eventual height of 6ft 4in, Freddie, too, might have become a giant in the Grasshoppers' line-out, but rugby didn't figure high up on his list of preferences when it came to ball games.

Cricket was always Freddie's number-one choice, and when he wasn't out playing it he liked to have his head stuck in *The Beano*. But the game at which Freddie first began to excel was, in fact, chess. His interest in the game was fostered by Mr Minter, one of the primary school's teachers, who organised a chess club that met during the school lunch break. It was something with which to occupy the kids when the weather was bad and they were unable to go outside.

Freddie was among a surprising number of youngsters eager to join the chess club, and he eventually became proficient enough to represent the schools of Lancashire, while his brother went on to play chess for England.

Years later, the cerebral Michael Atherton, graduate of Cambridge University, got a shock when he challenged Freddie to a game of chess. At that time, Atherton was the Lancashire captain and Freddie a relative newcomer on the County Cricket Club staff. His captain must have thought, He's just a big daft lad from Preston. This'll be a walkover, as they lined up the chess pieces on the board. To his surprise and chagrin, Atherton was annihilated.

Progressing from Greenlands County Primary to Ribbleton Hall High School, Freddie was disappointed to discover that cricket barely featured in his new school's curriculum. While the Flintoff family's home was situated in the smarter part of the school's catchment area, Ribbleton Hall drew a large proportion of its pupils from the local council estate, including some tough young lads for whom 'games' meant only one thing: football. Conveniently for them, the school felt that kicking a ball around was indeed the best way for the boys to expend their energy, rather than on a cricket field, where they might lose their wicket after a few balls and then stand idle for an hour or two at third man. Football, therefore, was the game played virtually all year round.

Being taller than most of the other boys and quick around the pitch, Freddie played soccer well enough to be selected to gain a game or two at centre-half for Preston schools, and also to turn out for Leyland St Mary's, but cricket was his consuming passion, and his enthusiasm for the game was shared by his brother, Chris, who was also showing great promise. They both received plenty of encouragement and coaching from their dad, Colin, the family rarely going anywhere without taking a bat and a ball with them. Blackpool was only twenty miles away, and on family trips to the seaside cricket on the sands gave the young Flintoff boys the added thrill of belting the ball into the sea.

At the age of eight, Freddie joined his dad and Chris to play cricket a few miles away from their home for local club Dutton Forshaw, which has since evolved into Harris Park Cricket Club, currently competing in the Palace Shield. Freddie played his first senior game for the club at Whittingham in the Loxham Cup when he was about eleven. The club's then president, Arthur Rose, recalls watching Freddie in the nets and noting how good he was for his age, particularly the way that, even back then, he drove anything pitched up and was into position quick enough to pull anything that asked to be hit – two trademark traits of Freddie's batting today. Though it was clear, even at that young age, that Andrew had potential, it was Chris Flintoff who covered himself in glory by establishing a Harris Park record score of 213, not out, which still stands today. The more academic of the two Flintoff boys, Chris might also have gone on to become a top cricketer if he hadn't chosen to go to university and become a teacher. Recently he has been teaching in Japan.

Given his school's preference for football, it was apparent to Freddie's family as he grew up that playing club cricket was the only way he would regularly get a game. 'Ribbleton Hall High was a football school, and there were only two cricket matches a year,' he says. 'The rest of the time was spent kicking a ball, so club cricket was very important to me.'

Harris Park had given Freddie a start but, as his talent began to blossom, it was imperative that he stepped up a level. It was generally felt that Freddie needed to stretch himself, and so he joined St Anne's Cricket Club, where he would benefit from regular professional coaching.

Based at the coastal resort near Blackpool, just eleven miles away, when it comes to sport St Anne's is usually more often associated with golf, with Royal Lytham and St Anne's being one of the best-known courses in the country. Even so, St Anne's Cricket Club also has a proud history that dates back more than 200 years.

It's thought that cricket was first played in St Anne's as early as 1870, and that the club was formed around a decade later. Some fifty years on, St Anne's was admitted to the Ribblesdale

Cricket League in 1927, and history records that in 1937 the legendary Syd Barnes – who regularly played for England between 1902 and 1913 and was revered as one of the best bowlers in the history of the game – turned out for St Anne's at the venerable age of sixty-three.

St Anne's remained in the Ribblesdale League until 1951, by which time the mushrooming of cricket clubs that had taken place after the Second World War now dictated that Lancashire's burgeoning leagues be split into sections. So, in November 1951, St Anne's became part of a newly formed Northern League, and proceeded to become undefeated champions in their first season. It has remained a notable Lancashire club ever since.

Freddie joined St Anne's as a twelve-year-old junior player in 1989 and soon worked his way up to play his first game in senior cricket for the Fourth XI as a thirteen-year-old. Graham Tindall, a much-respected servant of the club as player, coach and now chairman, remembers Freddie's debut vividly. 'A lot of the sides in Fourth XI teams were made up of eight or nine older fellows and two or three youngsters, but at our club we tended to be a little bit different and maybe had five older fellows and six youngsters. And on this occasion, Andy made his debut with his brother, Chris.

'Chris did some bowling, and they bowled the opposition out for about 50. Then our captain sent Andy in to open our innings with one of the more experienced batters to help the young lad. Andy was told to take it easy, to take his time and the more experienced opening bat would see him through. But they knocked the runs off in 8 overs and Andy finished on 38, not out. The other batter just stood there in amazement.'

There were occasional much-cherished occasions when the teamsheet contained the names of all three Flintoffs, with Colin lining up along with his two sons, but Freddie's progress was so rapid that by the time he was fourteen he had established a regular second-team place, playing alongside teammates much older than himself. Graham Tindall recalls, 'He made his debut as an opener playing away at Darwen, and there was a chap called Joseph who just stood at the non-striker's end, wondering what on earth he was doing there as the ball whistled past him and past the bowler's head.'

While playing in a twenty-overs-a-side game against Fordham Broughton in the Under-Fifteen National Club Cricket Championship, Freddie launched into an innings which is still talked about at St Anne's to this day. Incredibly, he smashed 234, not out, in an opening stand of 319 – an astonishing rate of scoring by any standard. The shocked schoolboy bowlers were hammered to or over the boundary with virtually every single ball. 'That knock by Freddie has passed into legend here,' says Russell Bradley, who played alongside him in the St Anne's First XI and is now Cricket Chairman at the club. 'It won't be done again, that's for sure.'

'Andy always had a lot of skill,' says Graham Tindall, 'and when I looked at him after he'd been here for twelve months, I thought, Yes, this lad has something special. But how far he was going to go in the game was another matter. You never know. You can have a thirteen-year-old or a fourteen-year-old who is very good at that age, and then they come to a block and don't really progress as much as you'd think they would.

'Andy had his problems when he was fifteen and sixteen. He shot up in height and had back trouble, and that didn't help him. But he was typical of a lot of lads at that age, because his back muscles hadn't strengthened. He had his trials and his tribulations along the way, but he came through all that.

'Andy's dad, Colin, was a good League cricketer and, luckily for them both, he was able to take Andrew around to matches. His dad was important to Andy, particularly in the early days, because he did need that parental support. But his dad was not one who interfered as a parent. When he came to St Anne's, he wasn't saying, "Our Andrew should be doing this" or "Our Andrew should be doing that." He let the lad develop in his own way. He was superb with Andy, very supportive, spending time with him and encouraging him without being pushy or demanding.'

Freddie had a spell in the seconds with St Anne's, where he played under the watchful eye of the club's then Cricket Chairman, Geoff Warburton. He, too, quickly saw Freddie's potential, not just as a batsman but also as a bowler, remembering how he bowled to a perfect line and length in a game at Morecambe and came up with various positive and intelligent ideas for field settings.

In 1992, at the age of fourteen, Freddie was considered good enough to be selected for the St Anne's First XI, for whom he made his full debut against Chorley, scoring 23. That season, he batted at number three in the order and St Anne's won the League, with Freddie often proving a match-winner. Coming in at first wicket down got him into the game early, and he proceeded to dominate bowlers with his fast scoring and ferocious hitting. 'You could always tell he was so much better than everyone else,' says Russell Bradley. 'You could always see he was a wonderful talent and well beyond anyone else in his age group. He always scored so fast.

'He took to first-team League cricket so much quicker and more easily than anybody else. But back then, the possibility of going on to play for Lancashire and England didn't seem to be on his mind much. Lancashire were obviously aware of him from quite a young age, but there was nothing much spoken about a career as a professional cricketer; he'd just come along and enjoy playing. We didn't see that much of his bowling because of his back, but as a batsman he could hit the ball a lot further than most.'

One famous victory, courtesy of a stunning Flintoff innings still revered and recalled fondly today by his old St Anne's teammates, was the win over Fleetwood, when a big not-out 100 from Freddie helped them to reach their target of 160 in 20 overs while only about 30 runs were scored at the other end.

That day, Graham Tindall was playing an away match for

one of St Anne's lower teams, but he was keeping an ear out for how the First XI were progressing. 'As we were driving back, we heard on the radio that St Anne's were chasing a total of 230 and had reached about 90 for 5,' he says. 'We just heard the score, nothing more, so we didn't know who was batting, but we all thought St Anne's had no chance of getting the runs going into the last 20 overs. But by the time we'd got back, we found it was all over: they'd knocked them off with 5 overs to spare. We found out that Andy had finished on 130. They told us he'd just peppered them, that he'd taken the bowling apart. And there were plenty of other games where he played like that.'

It wasn't only in the scorebook that Freddie left his mark. The number of shattered roof tiles that needed replacing on houses bordering the club ground bear testimony to the strength of his strokeplay and his penchant for striking big sixes. In the 1970s and early 1980s, part of the St Anne's sports grounds was sold off to developers, who set about building a housing estate on the land they had acquired. When mapping out the plots for the new homes, the planners obviously hadn't taken into account the prospect that one day the batting crease on the adjacent cricket pitch would be regularly occupied by a batsman with an ability to strike the ball such prodigious heights and distances.

'We had a third and fourth-team pitch at the back,' explains Tindall, 'and we sold that off to developers, which meant we were able to get funds to build a big clubhouse, which we were able to keep to a high standard. It also enabled us to spend money on the ground and improve the facilities, and now we have a nice clubhouse for our 1,200 members.

'Ours is a pretty ground with a big playing area, but it's not particularly long from behind each wicket to the boundary. Measured from the bowler's arm to the boundary, it's about probably fifty or so yards. So, from where Andy was batting in the middle, it was probably about seventy-five yards to the boundary. A lot of Andy's sixes were straight hits back over the bowler's head or over long on and long off. And they were really big hits. Behind the boundary at one end of the ground, there's a two-storey house with a high, peaked roof, and Andy used to hit the ball over the top of that roof, across the garden, across the road and on to the roof of houses on the other side. They were *big* sixes.'

Locals still talk with awe about Freddie's frequent aerial bombardments of their homes as bowlers were summarily despatched to all parts. And, of course, the retelling of these Flintoff exploits has grown ever more exaggerated in accordance with Freddie's elevation to the status he enjoys today as one of the world's best all-rounders and biggest hitters of a cricket ball. It's commonly told that one enormous six hit by Freddie soared over the ground's protective netting above the boundary, crashed through a window and smashed into a lavatory bowl – or on to some unfortunate woman's breakfast table, whichever version you prefer.

What cannot be disputed, however, is that Freddie made

quite an impact in every way with the residents during his years with St Anne's as he smashed balls over the road and into flower beds, or clean over the pavilion when he played at Blackpool's Stanley Park, a few miles away. 'It wasn't slogging but sweet timing,' points out former West Indian Test cricketer Eldine Baptiste, who was then the St Anne's overseas professional and Freddie's first captain at the club.

Because of problems with his back, Freddie's greatest achievements at St Anne's were with the bat, but Graham Tindall says that, when he did get the chance to bowl, Freddie was a handful because he was decidedly quick. 'He was very sharp,' he says. 'When Freddie eventually joined Lancashire, there was a chap called Jim Kenyon involved in coaching and, in particular, he was Warren Hegg's wicket-keeping coach at the county. And the word came back from Jim that Warren Hegg reckoned that, when Freddie was bowling, the ball went through to hit Warren's wicket-keeping gloves just as hard as anyone who bowled for Lancashire at that point. And Lancashire had Wasim Akram, who opened the bowling for Pakistan in those days. Make no mistake, Andrew was quick. If he really lets one go now, it's not far off 90mph.'

Tindall says that, when his fitness allowed him to bowl, Freddie was always eager for the captain to toss him the ball, always keen to be in the game. He displayed the same willingness as a youngster that marks him out today, says Tindall. 'In the last Test against South Africa in the recent series, he bowled on one leg because he was injured and he still bowled superbly. He was always willing to bowl when he was here, when his back allowed it.

'As a batsman, he was always very exciting to watch. There are a lot of players who struggle to reach the boundary all the way along the floor, but he could always hit the ball a long way, and now he's in a bracket of batsmen who empty bars. You can't afford to miss a Flintoff innings. And you wouldn't want to, because he plays shots that are just unbelievable.'

Freddie still maintains regular contact with Graham Tindall and others he played alongside at St Anne's; he hasn't forgotten where he learned his cricket. 'When he made his debut for England against South Africa, he gave us an England shirt signed by the whole England team,' says Graham. 'Last year we had a golf day and he came up and played, and he presented the club with one of his England sweaters.' Both shirt and sweater have each been framed and occupy pride of place on a wall in the St Anne's clubhouse.

'He's a smashing lad,' says Tindall, 'and we still keep in touch with him. I went out to South Africa for the recent Cape Town Test and, though I was just amongst the crowd, he spoke to me as though I'd seen him two weeks ago. He regularly pops down to the club at St Anne's, because his grandma and granddad come and watch our team here. Last year he came back off a tour and, although he had only a few days off, he popped down to see them and meet some of the lads he used to play with.

'He's just the same as he always was. I've known some young lads who have gone through and played county second-team cricket and they've got heads bigger than the whole of central London, but Andy hasn't. He hasn't lost contact with his roots, and I think that's helped him. He's a super person.

'He came to us at the age of twelve and played full-time until he was seventeen. Then, once he'd got a contract with Lancashire and had played five First-Class games, the rules state that you're not allowed to play in our league any more; you're only allowed one professional per team. So that was the end of him playing for us.

'I've been involved in cricket for many, many years, and it's the only time in my life that I've seen someone grow up and go on to the top of the profession. But the great thing is that he's still the same character. He's the same person he was as a young lad, and that's the biggest compliment I can give him.'

Russell Bradley echoes Tindall's sentiments. 'Andrew's a down-to-earth guy. He always was. There were no airs and graces about him, and he always got involved in the jokes in the dressing room. We're very proud he played for St Anne's.'

Freddie's deeds helped to elevate the stature of St Anne's in Lancashire cricket circles, and in return he remains grateful to the club for the chance they gave him as a youngster keen to improve his game. In 2000, he returned to St Anne's to play against his former club in an Ian Austin benefit match.

History relates that he left his mark once more in customary style, inflicting more damage on nearby roofs as well as causing a couple of dents in cars parked on the far side of the road beyond the houses.

Along with his club appearances for St Anne's in the Northern League, Freddie continued to play representative cricket for Lancashire after starting with the Under-Elevens at the age of nine in 1987. He played for the side until 1989, during which time he made an impressive 1,080 runs, averaging over 45 per match, and took 52 wickets at just over 7 runs apiece.

John Charlson, assistant manager of the Under-Elevens, recalls that back then Freddie's natural approach was just to hit the ball. 'Defence wasn't in his vocabulary, but he always had fantastic potential and he just got better and better. As I wrote in the end-of-year report, he could make the rest of the other lads look like schoolboys.'

The word inevitably spread around Lancashire cricket circles that there was a lanky teenager who looked to have the makings of a special player, and Freddie's progress was regularly monitored as he moved upwards through the various youth teams in the county's system.

Still, it wasn't all glory days. 'I went through patches of scoring runs,' Freddie remembers, 'but I scored mountains when I was in the Lancashire Under-Elevens, and I remember the 125, not out, I scored against Kent to this day.' Kent's boy bowlers took a pasting from Freddie that day at the Dartford

Festival. It was his very first century, earning him his first county cap from Lancashire, and he was so thrilled that he barely allowed it to leave his head for a week.

'By the time I'd graduated to the Under-Thirteens, I'd become more of a bowler,' Freddie continues, 'and I went through a bit of a lean spell as a batsman, coming in at number seven or eight. At nine, I was playing Under-Elevens, then Under-Fifteens and Under-Seventeens, as well as club cricket. I was playing every night of the week, and I loved it. I was tall and skinny like a rake until I was seventeen, and then I started to fill out. I used to get very worked up and fiery. I'm a lot more controlled these days.'

Joining Freddie in the Lancashire youth teams and also showing great potential was Phil Neville, now a Manchester United and England footballer. Freddie believes that Phil would have gone on to big things in cricket if he hadn't chosen a soccer career instead.

A tour of Argentina with Lancashire's Under-Sixteen side when he'd just entered his teens gave Freddie an early taste of playing overseas, and at fourteen he was thrilled to be selected to play his first representative game for his country in England's Under-Fifteens against Wales.

Also making his debut for England that day was Ben Hollioake, another tall and wiry all-rounder with the same fun-loving approach to cricket and with similar traits and credentials of being a hard-hitting batsman and medium-fast bowler. It was the start of a friendly rivalry and a firm friendship between the two which was to end tragically with Ben's death in a car crash in March 2002 at the age of twenty-four.

The match against Wales should always have been a memorable occasion for Freddie, but it's now remembered for all the wrong reasons. He was forced to leave the field with back trouble and seek an early appointment with a physiotherapist. It was the start of problems with his back that would intermittently dog his progress as an all-rounder over the next eight years as he rose through the England youth system to the full England side.

His England debut against Wales at the age of fourteen was, in fact, the last time for some three years that Freddie would turn his arm over competitively in a match. The muscles in his body were still developing, and they needed to be allowed to grow fully to support Freddie's tall, lean and gangling frame. At that point in his youth, they could not cope with the demands Freddie consistently made of them whenever he bowled.

Right from the very first time he ever marked out his run-up in a club match, Freddie had always been a whole-hearted bowler prepared to give it his all, but what he needed now was to be allowed to grow and fill out without imposing undue strain on his body. He was duly advised not to bowl, an especially bitter blow for a budding teenager whose cricket hero was Ian Botham for his charismatic batting and aggressive bowling for England. His other great cricketing idol was the wonderful West Indian batsman Viv (now Sir Vivian) Richards, who dominated bowlers as imperiously as any Test batsman ever has in any era.

Even in the past decade, great strides have been made in the devising and supervision of fitness schemes for youngsters aiming for excellence in sport. 'But there weren't any schemes in those days, monitoring the amount of cricket you were playing,' Freddie explains in a moment of quiet reflection. 'They didn't know the damage a child can do to himself, playing so much. I used to just bowl and bowl for hours on end. As one of the main players, they had me doing everything. I was called into the England Under-Nineteen squad when I was sixteen. They wanted me for my batting. So I went in at number nine and opened the bowling!'

Now, following the disaster against Wales, there was only one thing for it: Freddie had to forget about bowling for a while and concentrate on his batting until he was physically able to bowl again without risking serious and lasting damage to his body.

Freddie was still at school and was still only the tender age of fifteen when he was picked to make his debut for the county Second XI against Glamorgan at Lancashire's county headquarters, Old Trafford – a test not just of his ability but also of his temperament and maturity. It was yet another step up in level, and the opening bowling was as quick and hostile as anything he had faced to date. Batting in a borrowed helmet, he made a respectable 26 in the first innings and 13 in the second before off-spinner Robert Croft – a future England colleague – had him caught behind.

Playing for Lancashire's Second XI at Old Trafford might have fazed any fifteen-year-old, but Freddie says, 'I didn't feel any pressure whatsoever. I always believed that you just go out there and play your game. I'd already been playing for St Anne's in the Northern League, against seasoned Test pros, such as Kenny Benjamin. That did me so much good and really made me grow up.

'Playing good cricket at such a young age had a really positive effect. It means that everything is at a much higher standard, and it pulls your game up tremendously. Then, after the match, you can talk to some of the experienced players and learn from them.'

Captain of the Lancashire Second XI as Flintoff started to become a team regular was John Stanworth, who famously gave him his *Flintstones*-derived nickname. For the uninitiated, Fred Flintstone was the main character in *The Flintstones*, a classic American TV cartoon show first broadcast in 1960 and which ran for six years, eventually becoming in its day the longest-running animated American TV series in prime-time history.

The Flintstones was a parody on modern suburban life, translated to a Stone Age setting. The characters in the series all behaved and spoke in a contemporary manner, although they lived in the fictional prehistoric city of Bedrock. Fred Flintstone worked as an operator of a dinosaur-powered crane at the Rock Head & Quarry Cave Construction Co. (slogan: 'Own Your Own Cave And Be Secure'). At home in his split-level cave, Fred enjoyed such conveniences as a Stoneway piano and played his 'rock' records on a turntable, with a bird with a long beak acting as the needle.

Fred Flintstone, a big, burly bear of a man, cut a powerful figure in his leopard-skin tunic. He was larger than life, jovial and ebullient, and his antics on screen in search of mischievous fun appealed to all ages. Fred was a hugely popular sort of character, and very entertaining – qualities that apply equally to Andrew Flintoff.

For such a big man, Fred Flintstone had a soft side, which was never more touchingly displayed than when he was with his baby daughter, Pebbles. Equally, the soft side of Andrew Flintoff is never more apparent these days than when he is with his little girl, Holly, upon whom he dotes. All in all, he can hardly take offence at the nickname he's been given. It could be construed only as an entirely affectionate moniker when he was first given it, and it soon stuck. Fred rapidly evolved into Freddie, and the nickname has been embraced by many of his teammates, including England's captain, Michael Vaughan, as well as opponents, commentators and followers of cricket around the world, not least England's fanatical overseas travelling supporters, the Barmy Army.

Such is Flintoff's association with Fred Flintstone that, during England's 2002 appearances in India, a group of Barmy Army supporters led by a Welshman known as Mad

Dog clubbed together to buy a sizeable Fred Flintstone wendyhouse they had spotted in a Bangalore toy shop. Complete with a door, windows, an image of Fred Flintstone emblazoned on the front and the words THE FLINTSTONES imprinted on its sloping roof, the 'Freddiehouse', as it was swiftly renamed, was erected by the fans at the Bangalore cricket ground as the central point for the Flintoff fan club. Whenever Freddie – the Barmy Army's unofficial team mascot – came on to bowl or out to bat or hit a boundary or a six, the Freddiehouse was triumphantly held aloft to a chanted, football-style chorus of 'There's Only One Freddie Flintoff'.

The Freddiehouse itself, which can comfortably seat two inside when erected, has gone on to become a travelling symbol of support and appreciation, making its way on from India to New Zealand, where Nathan Astle, in one of the most explosive Test-match innings ever played, smashed one ball for six that hurtled into the crowd and straight through the Freddiehouse's front door. The house survived, and was again in evidence at the Tests during England's most recent tour of South Africa.

Paul Burnham, a leading light among England's Barmy Army, says, 'The England team spotted the Freddiehouse when it first appeared in the crowd in India, and they seemed to like it. Freddie, of course, is hugely popular, and the Freddiehouse is a nice focal point among the supporters when he's doing well.'

It's all good, harmless fun, and Freddie treats it as such. Indeed, on his official website, he can be seen wearing a T-shirt that fans can purchase and which has a Flintstone-style figure with a cricket bat tucked under one arm and a meaty palm tossing up a cricket ball.

Freddie remains Andrew, of course, to his family, but even august publication *The Times* forgets its stiff upper lip occasionally and refers to him affectionately on their sports pages as 'Freddie'.

Throughout his schooldays, all Freddie wanted to do was play cricket. Teammates frequently tipped him as a future Lancashire county player, but it wasn't something he'd especially set his heart on. Until that first appearance against Glamorgan for Lancashire's Second XI, cricket had essentially been just a game to him, a wonderful game to be enjoyed and played for fun. Now he realised properly for the first time that cricket could be a job and a career. It hadn't seriously occurred to him before, but he became so convinced that this was the path he wanted to follow that he wrote down 'professional cricketer' as his choice of profession in a careers form at school. He was told to think of a more realistic option but, thankfully for English cricket, this advice he steadfastly ignored.

Despite the amount of time he was devoting to his cricket, he didn't neglect his work in the classroom and gained nine GCSEs, all at either grade C or above. If he continued to keep up to speed with his work, there was no reason why he couldn't continue with his education, pass his A levels and then go on to university – no reason other than that the chance of making cricket a career was suddenly not just a possibility but positively beckoning. By now Freddie was sixteen and Lancashire County Cricket Club, under the busy and persuasive aegis of ex-Lancashire captain David Lloyd, were ready to offer Freddie a two-year contract to join their playing staff.

Lloyd, known affectionately throughout the game as 'Bumble' for the way he always seemed to be buzzing around with busy-as-a-bee infectious enthusiasm, went to watch Freddie for the first time when the youngster was playing for St Anne's in an away game against Leyland in the Northern League Division One on Saturday, 30 April 1994. All the reports reaching Lloyd's ears from Lancashire's youth coaches and officials about young Flintoff had been highly favourable, and Lloyd, as county coach, was there to cast a final eye over the young prodigy before officially offering him professional terms with Lancashire.

Freddie was aware that Lloyd was specifically at the Leyland game to run the rule over him and was desperately keen to make a good impression, but he was bowled in the very first over by Malcolm Marshall, the fine West Indian all-rounder who could propel a cricket ball twenty-two yards as briskly as anybody in his day. 'He was probably pretty disappointed, in view of the fact that David Lloyd was there,' says Russell

Bradley, who also played in that game, 'but if you've got to get out to anyone, then get out to Malcolm Marshall.'

Many a top-class international batsman had suffered a similar fate, but Freddie nevertheless couldn't help wondering if this fifth-ball failure in front of David Lloyd had damaged his chances with Lancashire.

In the event, he needn't have worried. Lloyd had himself been an opener who had played for England and knew what it was like to face the fastest new-ball bowlers in the world, including Australia's formidable pace duo Denis Lillee and Jeff Thompson on the Ashes tour of 1974–5. Coupled with previous reports of Freddie, he had seen enough in this one brief innings to convince him that Freddie should be offered the chance to join the Lancashire playing staff. The youngster, he noted, had appeared unruffled by Marshall's reputation; he hadn't frozen at the crease or been overawed as Marshall came bounding in, and Lloyd was impressed to see these qualities in one so young.

Lloyd, moreover, knew himself exactly what it was like to take guard, then have Marshall charging in at full tilt. He only had to cast his mind back to a One-Day International against the West Indies that he had played at Headingley in 1980 to know that Marshall could be a dangerous proposition. On that particular day, Lloyd had found himself leaving the ground in an ambulance after being hit on the point of his elbow by a lightning-quick Marshall delivery. So, losing his wicket so early in his innings to Marshall – who went on to take 6 for 36 that day – was certainly no disgrace for Freddie and no reason to change the generally held view at Lancashire that they should sign him up.

It wasn't long before Lloyd arrived at the Flintoff family home to discuss Freddie's future. Lloyd has always had an engaging way with words, a natural asset that has since made him a popular cricket commentator, as well as a much-sought-after and entertaining after-dinner speaker. Back then, sitting in the Flintoff family's front room, he stressed to Colin and Susan that he was confident that the youngster would make the grade. With typically spirited Lloyd enthusiasm, he persuasively outlined what he saw as a very bright future for their son at Old Trafford. Naturally, it was music to Freddie's ears.

Lloyd knew a thing or two about motivating young cricketers. He had enjoyed a glittering career as a professional in which he had scored 20,000 runs, including forty-three hundreds; played nine times for England, with a top score of 214, not out, against India; and had captained Lancashire for five years. He had gone on to become Lancashire coach after a brief stint as a First-Class umpire. Freddie was just flattered that someone who had made such a mark on the game as David Lloyd should be delivering his sales pitch to him in his front room.

Lloyd's offer of a two-year contract was difficult for Freddie to refuse, although his mother, Susan, had some misgivings. Her younger son's talent would require him to leave school and give up his studies in order to follow his dream. 'I can remember my mum wanted me to take a scholarship so I could go on to private school,' he says. 'In the end we decided against that, because I would have just been playing schoolboy cricket.'

There was indeed the possibility of a scholarship entry into Oundle School – a hopeful carrot dangled by Northamptonshire, another county who had been tipped off about Freddie's achievements on the cricket field and harboured hopes of enticing him to play for them. In view of the rapid strides Freddie had already made as a young cricketer, however, it was deemed that it would be a backward step for him to play public-school cricket in the school summer terms for the next two years while he studied for his A levels. Besides, it was always going to be Lancashire, not Northamptonshire, for Freddie.

With Accrington-born David Lloyd resolutely pointing out the benefits of playing for Lancashire rather than Northants, there was really no contest. Freddie's roots were in Lancashire, and the county had an illustrious cricket history of providing some fine players for England down the years. Maybe he could become one, too.

Freddie really needed no second invitation to sign on the dotted line for Lloyd. The alternative of two more years in a school classroom, studying for his A levels, when he could be playing the game he adored for a living must have made it a simple decision. For Freddie's mum, meanwhile, there was at least the consolation of knowing that, if things didn't work out at Lancashire County Cricket Club for her younger son within the next two years and he failed to make the grade, he would still be only eighteen years of age and could feasibly return to college, take his A levels and go on to university.

A few months spent working on the record counter at Woolworth's served only to convince Freddie still further that playing cricket was going to be his life. He enjoyed getting into the music at Woolworth's, but that was about the sum of it and he was grateful when a call-up for an England Under-Nineteens tour of the West Indies spelled the end of his stint as a shop assistant. The Caribbean was beckoning Andrew Flintoff; cricket from now on was going to be his life and David Lloyd was convinced that he was going to be a top player.

CHAPTER 2

Pros and Cons

'I remember my First XI debut for Lancashire so clearly, it's like it was yesterday. It was at Portsmouth against Hampshire, and I had a terrible match: I dropped three catches, got no runs, didn't take any wickets and finally broke down with a bad back.'

ANDREW FLINTOFF

It's not hard to imagine the sense of awe that Freddie must have felt the first time he arrived at Lancashire's magnificent Old Trafford headquarters as a fully fledged member of the playing staff. The ground is enshrined in tradition and steeped in history, and he was being given the chance – perhaps – to write a new chapter. Cricket has been played at Old Trafford since 1857, when Manchester Cricket Club set up home there after its formation at the beginning of the 1800s; and when the County Championship was constituted in July 1873, Lancashire was officially announced as one of the nine counties deemed to qualify for First-Class status.

Old Trafford's splendid museum reminds visitors and players alike of some of the great deeds on the field, dating right back to 1884, when Lancastrian Richard Barlow, playing for the north of England against the Australians, mastered the demon Aussie bowler Spofforth, who had arrogantly predicted that the opposition would be all out for 60. Spofforth's confidence may have been well founded; six years earlier he had taken 10 for 20 at Lord's and was largely responsible for a strong MCC side being bowled out twice in one day. But, in response to such pre-match Aussie sledging, Barlow defiantly hit a century at Old Trafford and took 10 Australian wickets into the bargain, prompting William Murdoch, Australia's captain, to take off his cap and present it to Barlow in appreciation of his efforts. Some believe that the phrase 'I take my hat off to you' originated with this gesture.

During the Second World War, after the ground was commandeered by the army, the pavilion and stands were badly damaged by bombing, which left vast craters across the field. Still, Old Trafford survived: the old pavilion was restored and the playing surface lovingly returfed.

Cricket heroes galore have graced the ground over the years since the first Test match was played at Old Trafford in 1884. Jim Laker famously took 19 Australian wickets in 1956 – still the best Test bowling performance – and Australian opener Bobby Simpson (who would later coach Freddie) struck the England bowlers all around the ground for a superb 311 in 1964.

Lancashire's proud contribution to England's cause includes some wonderful cricketers, with batsmen such as

Cyril Washbrook, Jack Ikin, Bob Barber and Geoff Pullar, and bowlers such as Brian Statham, Roy Tattersall, Ken Higgs and Peter Lever, to name but a few – and that's just in the last fifty years.

When Freddie first arrived at Old Trafford, the Lancashire team could boast a mixture of tough, seasoned pros and several big-name international cricketers like Michael Atherton, who was then England captain. Freddie had been at secondary school when Atherton had made his mark at international level; now he was a Lancashire player alongside him, along with Wasim Akram of Pakistan and Neil Fairbrother, a left-handed batsman who had played Test-match cricket for England and become a superb limited-overs player for both Lancashire and England. Also on the playing staff was John Crawley, a classy batsman who was starting to make his mark as an England player.

Freddie was noticeably shy in front of such accomplished stars and reticent to the point of speaking only when he was spoken to. Instead, he listened and tried to learn and absorb everything that was going on in the dressing room, in the nets and out in the middle. Neil Fairbrother, in particular, was especially willing to pass on his knowledge and advice, and generously made a point of going out of his way to keep an eye out for the youngster.

Freddie's reputation as a hard-hitting batsman had preceded him. When he first joined the Lancashire staff, stories abounded about his powerful strokeplay. He was clearly an exciting prospect and was being talked up as such by David Lloyd. But how would he fare when he regularly came up against bowlers a cut above those he had hitherto met? Just how good was he, technically? Did he have the technique to go with his strength, eye and timing? How committed was he? Cricket is littered with instances of youngsters making an early impact simply by virtue of being bigger and stronger than other boys of their age. They might be able to hit the ball harder and bowl a lot faster than others in their age group, but they might also be found wanting once their peers have grown up, too. It remained to be seen whether or not Freddie's raw teenage potential could blossom when he stepped up a level. And county cricket was a very big step, far bigger than he imagined.

A century for Lancashire's Second XI earned him an extension of another year on his two-year contract, and more big scores for the Second XI soon had him pressing in 1995 for a chance to play for the full county team. John Stanworth, then Lancashire's second-team captain, never doubted that Freddie would go on to become a first-team regular, because of his supreme natural ability. His only reservation was that it might take time for the full talent to flower, because Freddie had always taken time to find his feet at whichever level he had stepped up to. It was only when he felt settled in a side that he began to make the most of his talent.

By now Freddie had resumed bowling and had impressed everyone with his pace. Word got around that Lancashire's

Warren Hegg had to stand as far back to keep wicket to Freddie's bowling as he did to Wasim Akram's. And Wasim, who opened the bowling for Pakistan, was certainly no slouch and could hurry the best of batsmen.

Among those in particular who were championing Freddie's case for inclusion in the county side were Neil Fairbrother and David Lloyd, both of whom would provide loyal support – both together and separately – in different ways over the next decade and more: Lloyd as mentor, Lancashire coach and England coach, and Fairbrother as Freddie's agent, managing his professional life and commercial affairs.

During that 1995 season, Lancashire were prospering in the Britannic Assurance County Championship, despite Test calls for Atherton, Peter Martin, Mike Watkinson (who made his England debut at his home ground, Old Trafford) and John Crawley. By 14 August, Lancashire were just twenty-seven points behind the championship leaders with five games to go and with a game in hand. Disappointingly, they lost the next game to Yorkshire by 9 wickets, but they went to Hampshire for the four-day game starting at Portsmouth on 24 August still in the chase for the title.

At around this time, calls for Atherton, Crawley, Watkinson and Jerome Gallian to play in the Sixth Test against the West Indies once again weakened the side, which opened the way for Freddie to be picked to make his First-Class debut four months shy of his eighteenth birthday. He was understandably nervous when he took the field for the first time as a fully fledged County Championship player, but not because it was his debut; any nerves he might have had were because he was asked by stand-in captain Wasim to take up a fielding position at second slip after the Hampshire skipper Mark Nicholas won the toss and elected to bat.

Quite apart from talking Freddie up as a smashing batsman and an improving bowler, David Lloyd had frequently trumpeted Freddie around the club as a terrific slip fielder. 'Hands like buckets,' was how Lloyd liked to describe Freddie's prowess at slip. 'He could catch pigeons.' Wasim clearly believed him, but that belief had been completely eroded by the end of the day.

That morning, Wasim opened the bowling on a lightning-fast pitch and produced a masterly spell of swing bowling at fearsome pace, moving the ball both ways and at a speed Freddie had never experienced before as a slipper. On his first day on his Lancashire debut, Freddie missed three catches, including one that he saw and reacted to so late it was on to him before he knew it and the ball whacked him hard in the chest. 'It was one of the best spells of bowling I've ever seen,' Freddie reflected several years later. 'He was bowling at the speed of sound.' Fortunately for the lad who could supposedly 'catch pigeons' according to the coach, the misses weren't too costly; despite the spills at second slip, Wasim still managed to take 7 for 52 and Hampshire were bundled out for 154 in under 48 overs.

When it was Lancashire's turn to bat, Freddie went in at third wicket down and made only 7 before being caught off Heath Streak. In the second innings, Streak bowled him for a duck, but by then Lancashire were heading towards victory anyway. Freddie bowled 11 wicketless overs in the match for 39 runs, but he did manage to cling on to two catches in Hampshire's second innings. All in all, his County Championship debut had been a sharp – and bruising – learning experience, and he didn't play another County Championship match until 1997. Worse still, after the match he suffered more back trouble and once more was unable to bowl.

CHAPTER 3

Testing Times

'He has the potential to be a very good international player. I'd hate to see people label him as a superstar now, because it's difficult to deal with in someone so young, but he will be ready when the time is right.'

LANCASHIRE COACH DAV WHATMORE ON FREDDIE'S TEST SELECTION FOR ENGLAND AT THE AGE OF TWENTY

Andrew Flintoff was on the Lancashire team coach, travelling with other players to a benefit event for county colleague Wasim Akram deep in the Oxfordshire countryside in mid-July 1998, when an important call came through on teammate Mike Watkinson's mobile phone. It was from David Graveney, chairman of England's Test selectors, enquiring as to whether Flintoff was nearby and, if so, could Watkinson put him on the line because he, Graveney, had something of considerable consequence to say.

The players were all in jovial mood, and Freddie reckoned his leg was being pulled when Watkinson called out to say that it was Graveney on the phone, requesting to speak to him. Freddie still didn't believe his colleague was being serious even when Watkinson was insistent that he took the call and passed him the phone.

Watkinson knew that Graveney's call could mean only one thing: Andrew Flintoff was being called up to play for England. All eyes were on Freddie as he pressed the phone to his ear, and the youngster's polite expressions of surprise and thanks confirmed what everyone by now suspected: he had indeed been selected for the England squad – specifically, for the Fourth Test against South Africa at Trent Bridge, Nottingham, starting on 23 July. Graveney would have telephoned Freddie in person, but at that time the young player hadn't yet joined the increasing number of his generation with mobile phones. No matter how he got the message, however, it was the most exciting call of Freddie's young life and he jubilantly spent the rest of the day receiving handshakes, pats on the back and congratulations as the news spread.

To say that Freddie's selection was something of a surprise is an understatement. He never for one moment thought that he would be picked. He'd won his Test call-up after playing only fifteen County Championship games for Lancashire and had taken just 7 wickets. To some, it smacked of desperation on the part of the selectors, since Freddie's inclusion was the boldest of five changes made in a bid to revitalise an England side that had been outplayed in successive Tests.

England had enjoyed the better of the First Test, which had been marred by rain, but they'd been comprehensively stuffed in the Second Test, losing by 10 wickets in four days. They had even suffered the ignominy of becoming only the fourth team in Test history to record a total in which extras comprised the top score: there were 20 sundries, with Nasser Hussain's 15 runs being the next highest score.

Following this débâcle, England just managed to hang on for a gutsy draw in the Third Test after South Africa had piled up 552 for 5 declared in their first innings. But, having seen their team forced to follow on in successive Tests, the England selectors knew that something drastic had to be done in the Fourth to try and pull the series around. So they sent for Flintoff.

Making way for Freddie in the thirteen-man England squad in the position of batting all-rounder was his good friend Ben Hollioake, who had struggled for form during the summer. He had been selected for the squad for the Third Test but had been left out. Now Freddie was stepping up in his place, and Ben was among the first to offer his congratulations.

The irony for Freddie was that it had been young Surrey all-rounder Hollioake who had demonstrated to him that it was possible to break through into the top England ranks. His former England Under-Nineteen colleague had shown that Test-match cricket was in reach by earning a selection with his brother Adam in 1997. Ben had given Freddie belief. 'Watching Ben Hollioake doing so well – that was the real inspiration,' says Freddie. 'He opened the way and, as a result, we all believed that we could do it.'

David Graveney pretty much agreed when quizzed about Freddie's selection. 'All the selectors have been keen to get younger players into the atmosphere of Test cricket. Ben Hollioake got a taste last year. Now Andrew has edged him out.' He carefully did not say that Freddie was certain to play.

That summer of 1998, the sport that was dominating the TV screens was football, with all the drama of the World Cup unfolding in France. Although there was ultimately disappointment for England football fans, they had something very special to cheer about with the emergence of a teenager, Michael Owen, who scored a sensational goal against Argentina. Meanwhile, in the world of golf, another English youngster by the name of Justin Rose had burst through to make the headlines that summer. English cricket supporters, starved of success for so long, were soon praying that the youthful Andrew Flintoff, playing his first full season for Lancashire, would do for cricket what young Owen and Rose had done for their sports.

Poor crowds on some of the Test days that summer reflected the general view of the national cricket team in soccer-crazy Britain. England's cricketers hadn't won a major series for twelve years and, if English cricket wasn't exactly dying, it was dying for something spectacular to happen when the teams assembled at Trent Bridge with England one down and two to play, needing nothing other than a win if they were to have a chance of taking the series.

Although the selection of one as young, raw and inexperienced as Freddie might have looked like a desperate gamble, there was method to what many perceived to be the madness of the selectors. Tossing a twenty-year-old Flintoff, with such a limited First-Class record, into Test cricket was clearly a huge risk, but they weren't the first group of selectors to follow the adage 'If they're good enough, they're old enough.' They could point out that Ian Botham – to whom Freddie was inevitably starting to be compared – had been only twenty-one when he'd first been pitched into an Ashes series.

Moreover, Freddie had recently enjoyed a purple patch on the field in the weeks leading up to the Test. At the beginning of June he'd capped a memorable County Championship match at Northampton after scoring 46 in the first innings and following up with a career-best 124 in the second, an innings full of powerful strokes.

Soon afterwards, at Birmingham, he helped Lancashire chasing 336 to a fine win against Warwickshire by hitting 70 in 95 balls, including eight fours and two sixes. A bowling analysis of 3 wickets for 51 against Worcestershire was also a nudge to the selectors to take note of the options he gave to a team. Most importantly, he had got through a fair amount of overs without feeling any ill effects in his back. However, the knock that probably did most to earn Freddie his England selection was the blistering 61 he made in the second innings against Surrey in mid-June at Old Trafford – the fastest 50 of the season.

Freddie's sensational 61 was scored in a breathtaking blitz off just 24 balls, with seven fours and five sixes, and included smashing 34 in 1 over off his former England Under-Nineteen teammate Alex Tudor. The unfortunate Tudor also happened to bowl 2 no-balls, giving away a total of 38 in that over alone, which proved to be the most expensive in First-Class history (if you discount the 77 runs that once accrued in an over in New Zealand when Robert Vance continually bowled no-balls on purpose in an effort to contrive a result).

Happily for Lancashire followers, Freddie's extraordinary feat happened at Old Trafford on a Sunday afternoon in front of a bigger crowd than might otherwise have been the case for a County Championship match. The fans went home with something to tell their grandchildren.

It was Surrey's captain, Adam Hollioake, who gave Freddie the chance to show his paces, by making a declaration which asked Lancashire to score 250 to win off 53 overs. This became a target that Freddie ultimately made out to look not just generous but foolish. And yet Hollioake had no reason to suspect that Tudor would come in for such an astonishing battering. Tudor had, after all, taken 5 for 43 in Lancashire's first innings with some hostile fast bowling – and that included Flintoff's wicket for a duck.

Freddie marched to the crease in the second innings when the score was 151 for 2 in the 34th over and the match was in the balance. He quickly put down his marker by hitting the left-arm spinner Amin out of the attack before addressing himself to Tudor.

Tudor opened the over with a no-ball, watching it sail over mid-wicket for 6. It was such an effortless shot that even the young bowler couldn't help but inwardly admire it. Still bowling fast, but trying to adjust his length and line so that Freddie couldn't free his arms to strike big blows, the bowler watched his next three deliveries all disappear to the boundary for 4. Tudor's extra effort to put a brake on this blitz caused him to overstep once more on his 5th ball, and again Freddie whacked the no-ball away to the boundary. The next two deliveries were each dispatched for six, leaving the incredulous crowd baying for another six off the last ball to take the total for the over to an incredible 44. Freddie was all set to oblige, but somehow he played at and missed it, and with it the chance to compete with the records of Gary Sobers and Ravi Shastri, who had each hit six sixes off six-ball overs.

All of Freddie's massive blows during the over had been struck to the leg side, and one enormous six soared into the Kellogg's factory car park next to Old Trafford, a distance estimated to be fully 110 yards. The truly amazing scoring sequence for the 8-ball over was 6–4–4–4–4–6–6–0.

It was exceptional entertainment for the crowd, but what was pleasing for the purists was that these weren't cow shots, wild hoiks or merely the frenzied slogging of a part-time trundler; these were good cricket strokes played against a talented quick bowler. 'He was bowling very fast,' Adam

Hollioake protectively said of the bruised Tudor after the mayhem. 'Anyone who says there is no young talent in English cricket should come and watch these two guys.'

This memorable innings, coming as it did in the middle of a run of good form, inevitably made the selectors sit up and take notice. To David Lloyd, by now the England team coach, it was not altogether a surprise; he knew full well what Freddie was capable of and had been singing his praises for some time. First-hand word of Freddie's fireworks would also have reached England captain Alec Stewart via his battered Surrey teammates, even though Stewart himself had not been playing in the match because of Test commitments.

In mid-summer, Freddie had thus set out his stall as a wonderfully attacking player, and if the selectors were looking for an aggressive batsman, someone who would take the fight to the South Africans, then they could do a lot worse than pick him – which they duly did. Followers of England cricket soon had the appetising prospect of this young gun standing tall to take on South Africa's superb opening fast bowlers Allan Donald (nicknamed 'White Lightning' for his awesome pace) and Shaun Pollock.

Predictably, the popular press seized upon Freddie's size as they assessed England's big new hope. He was described as 'comfortably the biggest man playing professional cricket', and his physique was likened to that of an international rugby-union number eight or a heavyweight boxer. He was called a 'man mountain', weighing in at nearly seventeen stone, wearing size-twelve boots and loving Chinese food. One report said that, at his weight and height, he was probably one of the biggest players ever to be chosen for England.

Equally predictably, after the way he'd walloped Alex Tudor just a few weeks earlier, Freddie had to face up to numerous questions from the press as to whether he was 'the new Ian Botham'. To these he applied a commendably straight bat, saying that he didn't want any labels and that, however much he admired what Botham had achieved, he wanted to be Andrew Flintoff the first.

Captain Michael Atherton wisely concentrated on Freddie's talent, rather than on his weight or any comparisons with Botham, attesting that 'Andrew is the hardest hitter in the current game,' while Dav Whatmore, Lancashire's Australian head coach, commented, 'He has things he needs to work on, but he's learning very quickly and he gives the captain so many options. Quite apart from his obvious qualities as a batsman, he is a wonderful slip fieldsman, is superb at bat-and-pad and has one of the fastest arms in county cricket.'

While England were planning to introduce their latest young all-rounder to Test cricket, it was perhaps fitting that Sir Garfield Sobers – the greatest all-rounder of them all – should be the man called upon to officially open the new £7.2 million Radcliffe Road stand on the day before the Nottingham Test.

The following day, Freddie learned to his great joy that he was in England's starting XI. At the age of twenty years and 229 days, he became the youngest Lancashire player to make an England Test debut. In the same match, South Africa also gave a Test debut – to Steve Elworthy, who just happened to be thirteen years older than Freddie. On handing Freddie his first England cap and omitting bowlers Alan Mullally and Robert Croft, it was clear that Freddie would be expected to bowl on the first day after Alec Stewart won the toss and put the South Africans in to bat on a greenish pitch.

Walking out on to the field as an England player for the first time ranks as one of the proudest and most memorable moments in Freddie's life. There was generous applause when he was called up to bowl his first over in Test Match cricket to Daryl Cullinan, and he proceeded to display plenty of youthful energy and enthusiasm, eventually returning the respectable figures of 1 for 52 off 17 overs. He didn't take long to demonstrate a priceless knack of breaking partnerships, his first Test victim being the prize wicket of Jacques Kallis – whom he had caught at the wicket from a ball that cut back – after Kallis had added 79, for the 4th wicket with South African captain Hansie Cronje.

In answer to South Africa's total of 374, England made 336, with Freddie going in at number eight and making 17 in what *Wisden* described as 'a cameo of power and impetuousness'. Not for the first time, Freddie got out after aiming a big shot over extra cover, only to be caught at the wicket. Having got a start to his innings, the crowd and overconfidence got the better of him. He thus began his England career by losing his wicket to an overambitious stroke – a habit that was to become frustratingly familiar.

By bowling out South Africa for 208 in their second innings, England were left to make 247 to win. And if ever Freddie the debutant was to wonder what was really required – both mentally and in terms of commitment, not to mention technical ability – to become a top Test cricketer, then he needed to look no further than at a passage of play in his very first match that has passed into legend. It was the most thrilling and talked-about confrontation of the summer between two great cricket rivals: Mike Atherton and Allan Donald.

Freddie watched from the England balcony as Donald worked up a terrific pace, trying to dislodge Mike Atherton, whom many saw as England's best hope of a victory, provided that he stayed in to play a substantial innings. This unfolded into a classic duel of courage by a stubborn batsman against a fast bowler's fiercely sustained aggression and all-out effort.

When Atherton was on 27 he appeared to glove a catch through to the wicketkeeper, Boucher. But, as Boucher, the slips and Donald all went up in jubilation, Atherton simply stood his ground and the umpire remained unmoved. Donald was incredulous, and his fury spurred him into bowling as hostile a spell of vicious short-pitched deliveries as any England opening batsman has ever had to face. It was met by

Atherton – and by Nasser Hussain, batting with him – with unswerving bravery and defiant obstinacy. Atherton went on to make an unbeaten 98 and England won by 8 wickets.

Freddie, who wasn't required to bat in the second innings, thus found himself on the winning side in his first Test Match, but he went away from Trent Bridge knowing that he had an awful lot to learn before he could become not just comfortable at Test level but also good enough, mentally and technically, and not just to make a contribution to the team but to make a difference. The intensity of the Atherton–Donald duel had given him a glimpse at close quarters of what was required, both as batsman and bowler. It was quite unlike anything he had witnessed on the county circuit, and he recognised that he still had an awfully long way to go if he was to be a Test-match cricketer.

Freddie had come into the England side at a difficult time when several members of the team had been playing for their places against a strong South African outfit and when the England line-up had had one eye on being selected for the forthcoming tour of Australia. The focus, for some, was concentrated on their own game, and there wasn't much time or thought put into making sure that the young newcomer was made to feel totally at home and part of the family in the England dressing room. Freddie's natural shyness, also, didn't help him in that respect, and he felt a peripheral figure.

In his autobiography *Opening Up*, Michael Atherton recalled how, in what was hardly the most sensible piece of timing, a member of the England camp even tried to encourage a few basic adjustments to Freddie's run-up on the eve of the Test. Just as unhelpful, going into the biggest game of Flintoff's life, was a tinkering with the way he held the bat. Even so, while he might have felt something of a stranger that first time in the England dressing room, the selectors obviously felt that on the field he had performed adequately to retain his place for the series decider at Leeds.

The Fifth Test turned out to be a game to remember for England and their supporters, but one for Freddie to forget in terms of his own personal contribution. He recorded a 'pair' – a duck in each innings – and in the process learned another important lesson: even at Test level, with supposedly the world's best umpires officiating, you don't always get the right decision. In the first innings, in one of several contentious umpiring decisions during the game, he was given out, caught when the ball looked to have come off his pad. Although he bowled just 12 overs without taking a wicket, Freddie at least had the consolation of picking up a smart catch to dismiss danger man Jonty Rhodes for a superb 85 just when South Africa appeared to be heading fairly comfortably towards their required target of 219 to win the game after a disastrous start to their innings.

The match ebbed and flowed and moved towards a thrilling climax, which induced an extraordinarily loud and partisan crowd of 10,000 to turn out on the fourth morning to see whether England could take the 2 remaining wickets they needed for victory or whether South Africa could score the 34 they required to win.

In the England dressing room, before start of play, Freddie and the rest of the team were treated to some typically patriotic bravado from England talisman Darren Gough, effectively beating his chest and firing them up for the win. Within half an hour, it was all over, Gough duly claiming the last wicket by trapping Ntini LBW. England won by 23 runs, and within moments of the end of the match the crowd were thronging under the England balcony, watching their heroes spraying each other with champagne. Freddie had yet to make his mark as a Test player, and he looked slightly uncomfortable to be celebrating among his teammates after having bagged a pair and done nothing of note with the ball.

He might have scored just 17 runs in 3 innings and taken just 1 wicket for 112, but so far for Andrew Flintoff at Test level it was played two, won two.

To cap an unforgettable year, Freddie was settling into what was becoming a highly successful Lancashire side. He made important contributions in the Britannic Assurance County Championship and played in fifteen of the seventeen matches, missing out on two because of Test calls. He finished with an average of just over 26, was awarded his county cap and figured prominently in limited-overs games as Lancashire nearly completed an improbable treble.

After losing their first County Championship game of the

season, Lancashire never lost another all summer and finished runners-up in the competition. They triumphed in the Axa Sunday League and also won the NatWest trophy, which gave Freddie a brief taste of what it was like to play in a Lord's One-Day final. On paper, it looked likely to be an even contest with opponents Derbyshire, but rain caused the game to stretch over two days and Derbyshire were shot out for 108 in one of the most one-sided finals of all time, during which Freddie bowled just 3 overs but did manage to take a wicket. Lancashire knocked off the runs with ease for the loss of just Atherton's wicket, so Freddie never made it to the crease at the Mecca of cricket on that occasion.

Standing with Lancashire colleagues on the Lord's balcony at the age of twenty with Wasim Akram, holding up the trophy for the travelling fans to savour, was nonetheless an unforgettable and proud moment in the young cricketer's life. And the next day, Lancashire won the Axa League as well.

CHAPTER 4

Curry and Hits

'I suppose different people do things differently. I'm a very laid-back person. I don't know why but I never get nervous, even if it's a packed house at Lords. It's not because I don't care, or it doesn't matter, because it does.'

ANDREW FLINTOFF

Fanciful tales abound from cricket's post-War era of those swashbuckling cricket legends Denis Compton and Keith Miller. Great friends and international rivals, it's said that this flamboyant duo had a habit of turning up just minutes before they were due to take the field at the start of play with a girl on each arm, nursing hangovers and still dressed in the dinner jackets they'd worn to the party the night before.

However, those heady Compton–Miller days, when amateur cricketers played for the sheer fun of it and were known as Gentlemen, and professionals were known as Players because they were paid to play, had long gone by the time Freddie became an apprentice professional with Lancashire. Even for a player so naturally gifted, the demands of the modern game, as he quickly discovered, were markedly different – especially at the very top level. It takes more than a talent for hitting a ball a long way or bowling regularly at above 80mph to reach the top; it requires discipline, mental application, commitment, hours of practice, dedication to maintaining fitness and much else besides.

Freddie might have physically suffered more than his fair share of growing pains, but now, as a youngster with money in his pocket for the first time, he had to grow up in other ways too. When he left his parents' home in Preston and took a flat in Manchester, he was not unlike any other teenager spreading his wings. He was an affable, good-looking lad who naturally stood out in any crowd because of his height and size, and he soon became a target for the local girls because of his tall, fair-haired, athletic appeal and his fast-growing reputation as a sportsman.

One of Freddie's circle of friends at that time says, 'He certainly enjoyed a good night out drinking with his friends. He was popular with his mates and had an eye for the girls. Mind you, they had an eye for him, too. He was always generous to a fault with his money and was never backward when it came to buying a round or three of drinks. He was a really good bloke.

'He was a typical teenager back then, and enjoyed going out with his pals for a few pints and a curry, just like the rest of us. He'd been brought up very well by his parents in a solid family environment, and they were wonderfully supportive as he made his way with Lancashire. They regularly turned up to watch him play and give him every encouragement.

'But now he was away from home for the first time with a few quid in his pocket and was enjoying his freedom and a bit of the glamour. I think there was a time early on when his success went to his head a bit and he went off the rails somewhat – overdid the late nights and was his own worst enemy – but I think he would admit to that. In all fairness, he wouldn't be the first sportsman who had such fantastic ability that he thought he could just turn up and play and perform brilliantly after a hard night out. It took him a while to realise there was a lot more to doing well at cricket than relying just on his natural talent.'

Hugely popular with his mates as just one of the lads, Freddie enjoyed his favourite tipple (Guinness with just a dash of blackcurrant), could keep pace with the best of his pals and had a fondness for curries and other take-away fast foods, largely because it was simpler than rustling up something himself in the kitchen. But clearly there were days – and nights – of excess, and he has confessed that, in those early days spent living it up in Manchester, an average night out started at two in the afternoon. And Stuart Law, a Lancashire teammate and an Australian, recently wrote in the *Sydney Morning Herald* what it was like to be 'Freddied', as he described it. Law also ventured the opinion that Freddie might one day challenge the all-comers record set by Australian batsman David Boon of drinking fifty-two tinnies on a flight from England to Australia.

'Cricket's a team game, and when you've travelled with your

teammates halfway across the country, batted with them, bowled with them, fielded with them, won or lost with them, you're going to join them for a drink or two after the game on a Saturday night,' one cricketing friend points out. 'It's part of the camaraderie, and [Freddie's] mates understood that. But I think one or two of his girlfriends got too possessive and didn't appreciate that aspect of cricket. They resented it taking up so much of his time, particularly at weekends, which didn't make it easy for him.

'And, of course, when Freddie started doing really well, he'd be going abroad on tours for weeks on end, so it wasn't conducive to living the kind of settled, routine, nine-to-five lives that some of us lived. And at home he was pretty disorganised at times, to say the least; he wasn't the sort to have everything neat and tidy or filed away. It wasn't that he was sloppy about things because he was lazy or couldn't be bothered; that's just the way he was.'

Freddie, his teammates noticed, could be similarly disorganised in the dressing room. His jumbled kit would be spilling out in all directions from his kitbag and lockers, and this might have created the impression that he had a generally lackadaisical, undisciplined approach to his game and didn't care about it. And the way he got out after going for big shots, either too early before he had settled in or through sheer impatience or a rush of blood to the head and an unquenchable desire to hit the ball, tended to give the same impression; too often there were eye-catching big-hitting cameos and not enough innings of substance. The indication was that the commitment simply wasn't there.

Then, one famous incident after a Lancashire Second XI match showed unequivocally that the reverse was true. While playing against Yorkshire's Second XI, Freddie was livid with himself for getting out to a loose shot and, back in the pavilion, smashed his hand against a wall when his anger and frustration got the better of him. All he succeeded in doing was fracturing his hand, which put him out of action for several weeks, which in turn didn't please the Lancashire coaches. Word soon got around about Freddie's self-inflicted injury, but at least it showed that, contrary to what some might have believed, he cared deeply about his game.

'I suppose different people do things differently, and I'm a very laid-back person,' Freddie once said to explain his general demeanour. And he demonstrates this same attitude when waiting to bat. 'Until I'm next but one in, I'm sitting around in my shorts, very relaxed. When I'm next man in, I put all my kit on and start to take an interest in what's going on. It helps me to remain chilled, and that helps my game.

'Whenever I'm next man up to go into bat, it doesn't matter if it's a Test match or a county game in front of one man and his dog; I try to relax. Whatever people may like to imagine, I don't get pumped up. I don't know why, but I never get nervous, even if it's a packed house at Lords.' He went on to stress, 'It's not because I don't care, or it doesn't matter, because it does.'

While climbing the ladder with Lancashire, Freddie was

also playing regular England Under-Nineteen cricket and forging lasting friendships with teammates like Robert Key, Michael Vaughan and Steve Harmison, all of whom would later join Freddie in the full Test team. 'I went on three tours – West Indies, Zimbabwe and Pakistan – and played in home series against South Africa, New Zealand and Zimbabwe,' he recalls. 'That used to take up half of the season and, as a result, that kept me out of the county side. Becoming captain of the Under-Nineteens for two seasons had a major impact on me: it meant that I had to be much more responsible, and it might surprise some people but I really enjoyed it. I definitely had the feeling that I would like some more of that, not less. It undoubtedly helped my game, and eventually got me on to an England A-team tour, which did me the world of good. A lot of good players came through that route.'

On the 1998–9 England A tour of Zimbabwe and South Africa, Freddie proved to be the outstanding batsman in the England party, topping the batting averages with an aggregate of 542 runs at an average of 77.42. Particularly pleasing was the fact that he managed to bowl at a decent fast-medium pace and at such an economic rate that it earned him selection for England's World Cup squad. Significantly, he produced these fine performances on tour under the captaincy of a young batsman by the name of Michael Vaughan.

Freddie and the rest of the England A party flew back home in mid-March 1999, a time when interest in the forthcoming World Cup – to be played on home soil – was beginning to gather pace.

When assessing England's prospects, the media might not have singled out Freddie from the other fourteen squad players for special pre-tournament attention but for an afternoon of Flintoff mayhem inflicted upon Essex.

The Flintoff flame had flickered only fleetingly for Lancashire since he had first joined the county, partly due to constant international calls, and he was anxious to put that right as the new season got under way. As the reigning Sunday League champions, Lancashire Lightnings were equally anxious to get off to a good start against Essex Eagles in their first match of what was now a revamped One-Day competition called the CGU National League.

For the first time in any cricketing competition, the First-Class counties were now split into two divisions on merit, thus creating battles for promotion and to avoid relegation. In another innovation, each team would be allotted 45 overs, rather than the 50, 55, 60 or 65 that had been tried in tournaments of previous years.

This 45-over allocation, in itself, required a new set of mathematics for captains to conjure with when it came to setting totals and targets. It was therefore no surprise when Essex's skipper, Nasser Hussain – newly appointed England Test captain in succession to Alec Stewart – won the toss at Chelmsford on Sunday, 25 April and asked Lancashire to bat first, preferring to have a total to chase rather than a total to set.

When Lancashire slipped to 68 for 3, with England One-Day batting specialist Neil Fairbrother back in the pavilion for a duck, Hussain may have been well pleased with the way things were going for his side. Then enter Flintoff.

From his experiences with England, Hussain was better placed than most to know Flintoff's strengths and any perceived weaknesses in his game. He was fully aware of Freddie's threat with the bat but, with a decent attack at his disposal, Hussain was confident he could keep some sort of rein on him. His bowlers, after all, included former England paceman Mark Ilott; ex-England spinner Peter Such; England all-rounder Ronnie Irani, to bowl a nagging medium pace; and Ashley Cowan – who was being talked about as a possible England player – to open the bowling with Ilott.

What followed over the next hour and a half after Freddie strode to the middle, however, will be remembered for ever by those fortunate enough to have witnessed it – not least by Hussain himself and by his Essex bowlers, who must have felt at the end of it all that they'd walked into a hurricane. For, in the words of the *Daily Mail*'s cricket correspondent, Mike Dickson, Flintoff played 'one of the most electrifying One-Day innings ever seen'.

From the moment he came to the crease, Freddie gave notice that he wasn't intending to hang around. First, he proceeded to hit Stuart Law for three fours, and then forced Hussain to take Peter Such out of the attack by smashing him for two sixes in an over, one enormous hit sailing over the

Tom Pearce Stand frequented by Essex members before splashing into the River Can – a distance of well over 100 yards. It was a monster blow.

One-Day matches, by their nature, encourage batsmen to go for their shots, and the crowds drawn to One-Day games expect to see a few sixes. But, even by One-Day standards, this was developing into an exceptional display of big-hitting, and even the partisan Essex fans were on their feet as Freddie continued to batter the bowling out of sight. There was an excited buzz around the ground among the spectators as they sensed that they were watching something unfold that really was right out of the ordinary.

Watching Freddie's onslaught from his position at mid off, Hussain found himself powerless to stop the onslaught whichever way he swapped his bowlers around. They all came the same to Freddie, and they all went the same way.

His 50 came up off only 24 balls, out of 59 runs taken with his captain, John Crawley, who watched with admiration at the other end and wisely endeavoured to give Freddie as much of the strike as possible. It took Freddie just a further 26 balls to reach his 100, aided by an over from Cowan that included 5 balls despatched disdainfully to the boundary.

Typically, and thrillingly, Freddie entered three figures with another six, his fifth. It was his second off Paul Grayson, whom Hussain had called up to bowl in a desperate attempt to stem the flood of runs flowing so freely from Freddie's bat. Again, this milestone six was another massive blow that lifted a Grayson delivery into the Tom Pearce Stand, where it cannoned off the stand with such force that it imperilled one of the Essex fielders on the rebound. Incredibly, Freddie's 100 had come out of 148 runs scored in just 13 overs.

The Chelmsford crowd had never seen anything like it, and the blow brought all the spectators to their feet to applaud the opposition's number-five batsman. Soon they were ducking and diving for cover again as Freddie's amazing rampage continued.

Another huge six off Cowan landed on top of one of the hospitality tents beyond the long-on boundary. Pat Gibson, writing in *The Times* the following day, reported that Freddie produced 'strokes of such awesome power that not only the fielders but also the umpires were often in grave physical peril'. Gibson went on to note that during one delivery, where umpire Nigel Plews no-balled Ashley Cowan when he overstepped, 'It was probably the first instance of an umpire signalling a no-ball with his head tucked underneath his arm as the ball flashed past him to the boundary.'

Having reached his 100 in such brutal style, Freddie's innings was to last only another 16 balls, but that was time enough for him to club a further quartet of fiercely but cleanly struck sixes. These included one remarkable stroke where he nonchalantly contrived to make perfect contact, depositing the ball over midwicket, even though he'd taken one hand off the bat.

By the time he was out, in the penultimate over for 143

made off 66 balls in ninety-three minutes, Freddie had hit fifteen fours and no fewer than nine sixes – a total of 114 runs in boundaries alone. Four of his sixes came off Stuart Law, who had some sort of revenge by having him stumped as he tried to heave the bowler over the ropes at midwicket for a fifth six, having already smashed him for two maximums in the over. With Crawley, Freddie had put on 179 in 20 overs.

By any reckoning, it had been a truly sensational innings, a remarkable display of power-batting combined with sweet timing, and the Chelmsford crowd gave Freddie a standing ovation, applauding and cheering him all the way back to the pavilion. They knew they had witnessed a monumental and astonishing knock and the greatest cricket exhibition of big-hitting that they could ever hope or wish to see.

This, it must be remembered, was not a schoolboy or a Minor Counties attack that Freddie had so savagely put to the sword; this was the frontline Essex county attack, which had included three bowlers good enough to have played for England. All of them had been driven – literally – to despair. And repeatedly to the boundary, and over it.

Not content with this blitz with the bat, Freddie emphasised his growing worth as an all-rounder by having Essex opener Pritchard caught behind in his opening over, eventually claiming 3 wickets in the match, as well as pouching 2 catches for good measure to help Lancashire squeeze home by 3 runs. 'It was one of those days when everything came off,' said Freddie with modest understatement after his destructive knock. 'It's been an amazing last few months for me, and I can only hope things will continue to go my way.'

As an indication of what he might achieve in limited-overs cricket, given the chance, it seems faintly ridiculous in retrospect that England failed to get past the group stage of the 1999 World Cup largely because of an inferior run rate when Andrew Flintoff – potentially the most destructive batsman in the team – didn't get to face a single ball in three of England's first four matches.

England's net run rate and lack of urgency in routine wins over Sri Lanka, Kenya and Zimbabwe – without getting Freddie to the crease – left them needing a victory over India at Birmingham in the final group-stage game if they were to go through to the Super Six. In the event, they tamely lost, and suddenly they were out. It was the first time that England had failed to progress beyond the group stage of a World Cup, and the hosts were out of the tournament when it still had a further three weeks to run.

In that tournament, Freddie had been given very little chance to impress. And the fact that England failed to utilise his renowned ability for fast scoring in three of the games may have planted the idea in the mind of one light-fingered visitor to Birmingham that the all-rounder no longer required his bat; at the end of the game against India at Edgbaston, Freddie discovered it had been stolen from the dressing room.

England's World Cup failure prompted Alec Stewart to

resign as England's One-Day captain and David Lloyd to quit as manager, admitting, 'We have been found wanting when it really mattered.'

Lloyd's resignation came as a blow to Freddie, since the Lancastrian had been such a staunch supporter of the young player for so long. He must have wondered how he would fare under the new England stewardship of coach Duncan Fletcher and captain Nasser Hussain when he was included in the party for the tour of South Africa, beginning at the end of November 1999.

Johannesburg was the venue that marked Freddie's return to Test cricket for the first time in fifteen months. For Hussain and Fletcher, it marked the fourth-worst start in Test-match history when, in cloudy, damp conditions, England were reduced by top-class pace bowling from Donald and Pollock to 2 for 4 after just 17 balls. In the circumstances, Freddie's top score of 38 was a worthy effort, and he continued to make useful runs in the series until a foot stress fracture in the Fourth Test at Cape Town ended his tour. The new year was just two days old when Freddie limped out of the tour, dogged by yet another frustrating injury setback just when he'd been showing glimpses of coming to terms with Test-match cricket. It was the most depressing of starts to the new millennium, and back home on crutches he was left to ponder again on what might have been.

CHAPTER 5

All Right for a Fat Lad

'We've just watched one of the most awesome innings we're ever going to see on a cricket field.'

FORMER ENGLAND CAPTAIN DAVID GOWER ON FREDDIE'S MATCH-WINNING INNINGS OF 135 NOT OUT AT THE OVAL ON 26 JULY 2000

It's probably safe to say that, when WG Grace was in his pomp, no spectator dared to cast aspersions about the great man's ample girth by shouting mockingly from the boundary, 'Who ate all the pies?'

Of course, there have always been Test cricketers with less-than-sylphlike figures whose generous waist measurements have attracted jokey comments from the crowd, such as England's Colin Milburn and Australia's David Boon, both of whose fleshy frames could be kindly described as 'well built'. And then there was Australia's moustachioed pace bowler Merv Hughes, who cheerfully endured regular taunts of 'sumo' towards the end of his Test career in the early 1990s.

But surely no international cricketer has been so publicly humiliated for his poundage as Andrew Flintoff was in the summer of 2000. An unwise choice of diet, combined with further problems with his back that prevented him from training as much as he might have done, had seen Freddie's weight increase just at a time when he also appeared to be failing to fulfil his obvious potential.

The worry within the England camp about Freddie's weight began somehow to filter into the newspapers. The implication was that there were some in the England hierarchy (no names were mentioned) who considered that he wasn't doing himself justice at international level because he was being unprofessional with his fitness. It was as much a whispering campaign against him as anything else, as there was no official reprimand.

The storm broke in the newspapers after Freddie had got out to an apparently careless slog in a One-Day International against Zimbabwe which England lost by 5 wickets. Soon Freddie's bulk was a hot topic on the back pages and, however much he tried to ignore it, it nevertheless hurt him deeply. One newspaper even ran a tale-of-the-tape comparison with heavyweight boxing champion Lennox Lewis and decided that, at nineteen stone, Freddie was even bigger than the boxer.

The abusive headlines truly horrified Freddie, and the debate in the newspapers made for miserable moments fielding on the boundary, close to spectators who chose to continue the debate with their own unflattering brand of adjectives. 'Who ate all the pies?', a favourite among football fans for any member of the opposing team perceived to be carrying even an ounce of surplus flesh, was one of the milder taunts he had to endure.

Freddie was conscious that he needed to lose weight, but such personal abuse was hard for him to take. He could accept criticism if he had bowled or batted poorly, but he found the headlines about his weight especially embarrassing for his family, particularly his mother and father, and it had such an effect on him that for a while he chose to stay at home whenever possible. If he ventured out, he felt self-conscious and wondered if everyone was looking at him, sizing him up.

It's a tribute to Freddie's strength of character that he answered his critics in the best possible way: on the pitch. The fuss about his weight was still making news when he smote a rapid 42, not out, off 45 balls to help England crush Zimbabwe by 8 wickets in a day–night One-Day International at Old Trafford on 13 July. His performance earned him the Man Of The Match award, and after the presentation he commented tellingly that he'd done 'all right for a fat lad'.

Nearly two weeks later, Freddie was still receiving abuse about his weight hurled by a group of rowdy spectators when he played for Lancashire in a vital NatWest Trophy match against Surrey at the Oval. Jeers, catcalls and shouts about the pitch not needing the heavy roller greeted him when he came on to bowl first change, and the remarks were still flying when he came out to bat. 'Fat Freddie' was the chant from the particularly vociferous bunch, mixed in with a few less polite Anglo-Saxon adjectives also beginning with F.

Freddie came to the wicket almost at the start of the Lancashire innings, replacing Atherton, who had been bowled for a duck. He let his bat do the talking for him and proceeded to ram the taunts of his abusers straight down their throats, right from the word go. His first ball was a leg-side half-volley, which he despatched to the boundary, and it set the tone for a quite exceptional innings. When the bowlers pitched up, their deliveries were driven like a bullet for four. When they pitched short, they disappeared over the rope. Even Freddie's verbal detractors could scarce forbear to cheer. The mocking remarks gave way first to silence and finally to acknowledgement that they were watching a thrilling innings of immense character. After racing to his 100 in 88 balls, Freddie made an exaggerated bow in the direction of the noisy bunch, then went on to reach 135 not out in 111 balls, rushing Surrey to defeat by 8 wickets. With Ganguly, Freddie knocked up 190 – a record for Lancashire's second wicket in the competition. On witnessing the match-winning innings, former England captain David Gower declared, 'We have just watched one of the most awesome innings we are ever going to see on a cricket field.'

Among the crowd that day, enthralled by Freddie's blitz and the way he had emphatically silenced his verbal offenders, was MCC member Simon Kinnersley. Later, Freddie explained to him just how much the recent taunts had affected him.

'Getting barracked and having the crowd chanting, "Who ate all the pies?" was embarrassing,' he conceded, 'especially when your family are there to watch. I found that the best way of dealing with those kind of remarks was to ignore them. I knew very well that I couldn't do an Eric Cantona and pile into the crowd, so it was better not to listen.

'Also, quite often it was some bloke who weighs twenty stone and who was guzzling food all day long who was dishing it out, and it was quite obvious that they had never done a stroke of exercise in their lives. And yet there they are, giving you all this grief. It's just sad.

'I've just learned not to read or listen to what's being said about me. Imagine if I lost a lot of weight; the next thing, there'd be headlines saying, "Freddie's Anorexia Fear!" I don't mind criticism when I've played a bad shot – that's merited – but I do mind being picked to pieces because of the way I look. When that was at its worst, I shut myself off and lived like a hermit for a while.'

Frustratingly for Freddie and the England management, the flashes of brilliance he'd showed at the Oval that day proved too infrequent, and yet there were days when he could be a simply magnificent match-winner. At Karachi, on England's winter tour of Pakistan, he scored a scintillating 84 in 60 balls to help England successfully chase down a target of over 300 for the first time in a One-Day International. The innings was all the more remarkable for the fact that it came five days after he had learned that back problems would prevent him from fulfilling the all-rounder's role in the Test team. The sad fact was that he would miss the next seventeen Tests.

All too often, Freddie had flattered only to deceive with his batting, and his intermittent back problems made it difficult for him to be reliably considered as an all-rounder. By the end of the following summer, his cricket career had reached a crisis point. Exasperated by the fact that he was failing to fulfil his potential and make the most of his natural gifts, England dropped him. Looking back, Freddie understands why. 'I was just rubbish. I was lucky to be playing for Lancashire, never mind England.' There was even talk of Freddie leaving Lancashire for another county to make a new start. This rumour later proved unfounded, however, and Freddie signed up with Lancashire for another five years in 2001 – but only after a tough triumvirate turned his life around.

The credit for rescuing Freddie's career from oblivion goes to three different men, all of whom were close to him and weren't afraid to tell him a few home truths for his own good. First, Bobby Simpson, a former Australian captain and then Lancashire coach, gave him a typically frank Australian character assessment, which left no room for misunderstandings. Simpson basically told Freddie that he was a fool for betraying his talent by playing the way he was, except he didn't use the word *fool.*

Then, on 16 September 2001, as another indifferent season drew to a close, Freddie was taken aside in the Lancashire dressing room by his good friend and Lancashire and England colleague Neil Fairbrother, in company with Chubby Chandler, who had become Freddie's manager. Following Bobby Simpson's lead, they together gave him a similarly forceful dressing-down.

Fairbrother, in particular, had proved a trusted friend to Freddie in Lancashire and England colours right from his earliest days as a Lancashire professional. If anyone could get the message across to Freddie that it was time to mend his ways, it was Fairbrother. By this time Freddie's agent, he and Chandler didn't mince their words, and together the three of them worked out various ways for the youngster to get his game back on track. They called for him to show more commitment, to be more professional in his approach, to pay more attention to what he ate and drank and to his general fitness. They stressed that he would need to demonstrate dedication, a willingness to practise more and a change of attitude.

The effect was almost immediate. Freddie resolved to cut out the junk food, took care as to what and how much he drank, started to lose weight and took it upon himself to telephone Duncan Fletcher to ask if he could go to the Academy in Australia, where England's young hopefuls were taken on with the object of toughening them up for international cricket.

Importantly, the Academy set great store in developing the mental toughness needed in young cricketers to perform at the highest level. They considered the right approach and attitude vital. Originally, Freddie wasn't among the players selected for the Academy party, and Duncan Fletcher can't fail to have been impressed by Freddie's call, asking if he could be included at his own expense. It demonstrated to the England coach that Freddie did indeed care enough about his game, and that he was now prepared to put in the hard work to improve it.

For the England management, it was a welcome gesture of intent. For Freddie, it was the first step on a make-or-break cricket journey. Within months, he would score his first Test century and newswires would flash around the world from India an unlikely image of Flintoff the hero, cavorting half-naked down the pitch in a packed Indian stadium after tearing off his shirt.

CHAPTER 6

Triumph and Sorrow

'I don't think St Anne's would have trusted me with the final over a year ago, let alone England.'

ANDREW FLINTOFF AFTER BOWLING ENGLAND TO VICTORY WITH THE PENULTIMATE BALL IN THE SIXTH ONE-DAY INTERNATIONAL AGAINST INDIA IN MUMBAI ON 3 FEBRUARY 2002

Sometimes you make your own luck. Freddie's decision to book into the National Academy in Adelaide of his own volition not only kept him working at his fitness and his game but also kept his name in the thoughts of Hussain and Fletcher on England's subsequent tour of India in the winter of 2001. The captain and coach would never completely lose faith in Freddie at any stage, but one paragraph in Hussain's autobiography, *Playing With Fire*, sums up the mountain Freddie had to climb if he was to get back in favour. 'At that time I wished I had a Jiminy Cricket I could perch on Freddie's shoulder to tell him what to do all the time, because he didn't do himself any favours in the early years of his England career. His preparation was terrible. His netting was unprofessional. No wonder he wasn't fulfilling his vast potential at this stage.'

It was therefore an act of faith when the England management called up Freddie after the first tour match in India as cover for Yorkshire all-rounder Craig White, who had come to the realisation that, while he could still turn his arm over, injury would prevent him from bowling at full pace. White's setback was hardly the best of starts to England's first tour of India for nine years, but it did offer Freddie a way back into the England set-up. Reports from the Academy, where Freddie had been getting up at six o'clock every morning as part of a strict regime, had been encouraging, and so he was told to get on a plane to India as soon as possible.

Already missing regular pace bowlers Andy Caddick and Darren Gough, England's most pressing need was for Freddie's ability to bowl fast and bang the ball in hard on the Indian pitches. After arriving towards the end of November 2001, he was thrust straight into England's next match, against India A, as an opening bowler. A total of 34 overs in the match proved his fitness, while 6 wickets proved his effectiveness in alien conditions.

By the time the Second Test at Ahmedabad came around, Freddie had done enough for Hussain to entrust him with the new ball in his hands to open the attack with Matthew Hoggard for the first time in a Test. Nor did Freddie let anyone down, taking 2 for 42 in 22 tidy overs in India's first innings, including the wicket of captain Ganguly – a much-prized scalp of a former Lancashire colleague.

While Freddie could be pleased with his bowling as the

three-Test series progressed, his batting was nothing short of a disaster. Hopelessly tied up in knots by the Indian spinners, he scored a miserable 26 runs in 5 innings, including two ducks. It was torture for followers of English cricket to see such a fine striker of a cricket ball being repeatedly tormented by Anil Kumble's leg-breaks and Harbhajan Singh's floaters. Freddie never looked like surviving an over, let alone making any runs. Worse still, he was batting at number six in the order, which left England with a very hollow centre.

Freddie was in utter despair. He had returned to the England fold much fitter, full of hope and considerably lighter, yet he couldn't even buy a run. The disappointment finally got to him after recording his second duck in his string of five failures, during England's first innings in the Third Test at Bangalore. There he lasted only four balls and got out by naively hitting a catch to midwicket just at a time when England were looking for someone to steady their innings. Back in the dressing room, he could contain his frustration no longer and broke down in tears.

Recounting this lowest moment of his career in an interview with the *Observer Sport Monthly*, Freddie recalled, 'I'd started turning it all around. I'd been on the Academy, I'd lost weight, I was bowling, I was working hard, but I couldn't score runs for love nor money. It just wasn't happening, and from there everybody says: "You can't bat against spin. You can't do this or that. You can't bowl anyone out." It got to the point in Bangalore where I didn't know what to do, so I put a towel around my head and shed a few tears. Graham Dilley [then the England bowling coach] put his arm around me and chatted about something else, away from cricket. Then I think I went out and took four wickets, which eased the pain a bit.'

Once again, Freddie showed commendable 'bounce-backability', to use a modern term beloved of sports commentators. After his fifth abject failure with the bat, he took the new ball and ripped out the first 3 Indian wickets at a personal cost of 30 runs, which left him feeling a good deal better. He finally finished with what were then his best Test figures to date: 4 for 50 in 28 hostile and economical overs. He also impressed those who mattered in the England camp by bowling with heart and skill to a plan designed to restrict Sachin Tendulkar's prodigious talent; Freddie was frequently asked by Hussain to come around the wicket and bowl outside the leg stump to India's master batsman.

Freddie was rewarded for his efforts with the ball by being named Man Of The Match at the conclusion of the Third Test, a much-needed boost to his confidence and a timely slice of good cheer with Christmas just two days away.

Still to come on England's tour of India after the festive break were six One-Day Internationals, and again it was Freddie's bowling, rather than his batting, that proved more of an asset to the England team, although he contributed an important half-century in the fifth match, which helped England to squeeze home by two runs. England had thus clawed their way back from a three–one series deficit and now needed to win the final game at Mumbai to square the series.

India's fans are some of the most impassioned supporters in world cricket, and some 60,000 of them turned out at the Wankhede Stadium on 3 February 2002 for the day–night game to will their team on noisily to a victory that would clinch the series. After already losing the Test series, England were desperate to finish on a winning note in the limited-overs form of the game. A drawn series from three–one down would be a considerable achievement.

England's chances looked anything but promising when they collapsed to 174 for 7 after 30 overs, but Freddie made an invaluable 40 and took charge of the tail to push the total up to a challenging 255, which included a priceless 37-run partnership with Darren Gough for the last wicket.

India appeared to be on course for victory, thanks to a blistering 80 from Ganguly, and although their middle order faltered they were still favourites to win by the time Hussain tossed the ball to Freddie to bowl the final over. The tension was unbearable, and in front of a baying crowd the target came down to 6 runs to win in 3 balls. This became 6 in 2 when Freddie ran out Kumble with a neat piece of footwork, side-footing the ball on to the stumps. The noise from the Indian supporters in the stadium reached a raucous climax, fireworks were exploding and the atmosphere was electric. Then, with the game's penultimate ball, Freddie ran in and knocked over last man Srinath's stumps. England had won a dramatic victory, and Freddie had spoiled the party for 60,000 spectators.

The moment he saw the ball beat Srinath's flailing bat and shatter the stumps, Freddie tore off his shirt in uninhibited jubilation and relief and careered down the pitch, chased by his delighted teammates. 'It was a massive release of tension,' he later said of this sweet moment, 'but after about ten seconds of running round, waving my shirt, I asked myself, "What are you doing?" I had the whitest, palest body in the world, and there were about 60,000 Indians there.'

Freddie's wonderfully exuberant reaction reminded many of a similar moment of exultation from Ryan Giggs, who whipped off his shirt and whirled it around his head after scoring one of football's greatest goals for Manchester United against Arsenal in an FA Cup semi-final at Villa Park in the year United famously won the Treble.

As with Giggs, no one could seriously begrudge Freddie his ostentatious moment of triumph, although it earned him a mild but obligatory rebuke from management. Significantly, no fine was forthcoming, but soon afterwards Freddie got a dressing-down from his dad. Colin Flintoff had telephoned to congratulate his son on his efforts, but he was moved to add a fatherly word of advice on sartorial etiquette when playing cricket for one's country. Soon, pictures of a topless Freddie with a huge, beaming smile on his face, being mobbed by his teammates, made sports pages all over the world. The nineteen-stone Freddie of yore would never have laid his torso bare for such inspection by photographers and TV cameras and, even if he wasn't yet down to his target of sixteen-and-a-half stone, it was nevertheless another sign of his growing belief in himself. In an interview after the breathtaking finale to the game, he said – as modest as ever – 'I don't think St Anne's would have trusted me with the final over a year ago, let alone England.'

It was a reminder – to himself as much as anyone – of how far he had come in a few short months. When he'd volunteered for the Academy, he'd had no idea he'd be reclaiming his England spot quite so soon, but he'd seized his chance, made important contributions with both bat and ball and was increasingly confident that he had what it takes to compete at the top level.

As the team prepared to move on to New Zealand, Freddie's progress and the dedication he'd shown weren't lost on Duncan Fletcher – nor on Nasser Hussain, who commented, 'I'm a big fan of Flintoff and his attitude in the last few months. He's done the hard work and now it's paying off. He is important to English cricket as the one person who can do things that others can't.'

CHAPTER 7

Breakthrough

'He misses Ben Hollioake terribly. They were always great together: Ben the elegant ladies' man – a bit suave, self-deprecating – and Freddie the down-to-earth, full-of-beans lad from the northwest of England.'

DR DAVID ENGLISH, MBE, VICE-PRESIDENT OF THE ENGLISH SCHOOLS CRICKET ASSOCIATION

It's Andrew Flintoff's misfortune that the First Test between New Zealand and England at Christchurch in March 2002 is remembered not for Freddie's electrifying maiden Test 100 but for the performance of Kiwi Nathan Astle in one of the most astonishing Test innings of all time. Freddie's powerful milestone knock of 137, after collecting a duck in the first innings, was overshadowed by Astle smashing the fastest double 100 in Test history, in the process bringing New Zealand within sight of one of the most wildly improbable victories ever.

For English cricket, however, the match can be regarded as the one in which Freddie demonstrated at last that he could make big runs at Test level. Until then, his Test best had been 42, and he came to the crease at Wellington second time around after having accrued a paltry total of 8 runs in his previous 5 Test innings. It can be safely said that he owed the England team a decent score – and they certainly needed one when he joined Graham Thorpe, with England tottering on 106 for 5, leading by just 187.

From the start Freddie oozed confidence, middling the ball straight away and racing to 26 in his first 13 balls. The boundaries soon started to flow from his bat, while the experienced Thorpe regularly gave him encouragement and the benefit of his vast experience between overs. England needed plenty more runs from the pair before they could consider themselves out of the woods, and Thorpe was anxious that his partner would not give his wicket away. He was also desperate to see Freddie through to his maiden Test 100 after his repeated failures with the bat in India. When Freddie moved into the 80s, the Surrey left-hander walked down the wicket and reminded Freddie of how he had felt in India when he couldn't score a run, and yet here he was now with a great chance of a century if he showed patience and selected the right ball to hit.

Freddie had moved on to 98 when, after ignoring several short-pitched tempters from the New Zealand bowlers, he could restrain himself no longer. Along came a bouncer from McMillan that he couldn't resist, and he went for the hook. He top-edged the shot, but fortunately for Freddie the ball flew over the wicketkeeper's head to the boundary.

After all his injury problems, his battles with his weight and troubles of his own making, it was a sweet moment greeted with generous applause from the crowd – not least from the Barmy Army contingent, grouped around the Freddiehouse – and a hug of congratulations from Thorpe. Even though the scoreboard told him he had reached triple figures, it didn't really sink in for Freddie until he went in at tea to be greeted by an ecstatic Warren Hegg, spelling out to him that he'd made a Test century.

Freddie's 100 arrived in 114 balls, and with Thorpe – who made 200, not out – he put on 281, a record for England's sixth wicket. After hoisting three figures on the scoreboard, Freddie returned after tea to play with increased freedom and was eventually out for 137.

Freddie's ton helped to set up a total of a massive 549 for the Kiwis to chase. The match looked as good as over for England when their opponents were reduced to 333 for nine, but Nathan Astle then gave the England team the fright of their lives by launching into a ferocious assault on all the England bowlers, flaying them all and – incredibly – taking his score from 101 to 200 in just 39 balls. In all, he smashed 222 runs, including eleven sixes, and looked capable of pulling off a truly astonishing victory until Hoggard finally had him caught behind with New Zealand still 98 runs short.

Congratulations poured in for Freddie from all quarters for what was perceived as the big man's breakthrough innings after years of underachievement. His maiden Test ton in a hard-earned England victory prompted him to enjoy some serious celebrations in a bar in Christchurch with some of the other England players before the team moved on to Wellington to prepare for the Second Test. But absolutely nothing could prepare them for a tragedy in the middle of the Test that was to leave the team – and Freddie in particular – devastated.

England's first innings was under way at Wellington's Basin Reserve, and Freddie had his pads on as next man in, when he heard the terrible news that Ben Hollioake had been killed in a car crash in Perth, Western Australia. Driving back late at night after a family meal, the young cricketer had been killed instantly at the wheel of his black Porsche 924 when it left the road and crashed into a wall. He was just twenty years and 132 days old, and no England cricketer had ever died at such a young age.

Ben's tragic death came as a terrible shock not just to the England party but also to everyone in the cricket community, and it immediately rendered events on the field at Wellington utterly insignificant. Always a popular figure among his colleagues for his relaxed, easygoing nature, just a few weeks earlier Ben had been in England's dressing room as part of the One-Day squad. The players could scarcely take in the reality of what had happened.

For Freddie, Ben's death was the loss of a close friend he had known since he was eight. Together they had played England representative cricket throughout their schooldays, and Ben had done well under Freddie's captaincy in England's Under-Nineteen team in Pakistan in 1996–7.

Dr David English, MBE, recalls noting the strength of the friendship that had developed between the pair while they were both still in their early teens. 'I remember they got on so well when they were together at the 1992 Bunbury Schools Festival, at Charterhouse, along with Alex Tudor, Gareth Batty and Steve Harmison. Freddie was tall and thin then, very much like Ian Botham in that he had enormous self-belief, was one of the boys, very generous as a player, a great team man, smashed the ball miles and bowled like a whirlwind. Both he and Ben had so much talent and enthusiasm, and they were very kind to the players around them. I always remember them helping and encouraging.'

Like Freddie, Ben received an early call-up for England and hit a brilliant 63 off 48 balls in a One-Day game against Australia at Lord's when he was only nineteen. Like Freddie, he was tipped for a great England future, but, like Freddie, he spent the next few years not quite fulfilling his golden talent. He and Freddie had batted together, bowled together, toured together and vied with each other for an England place. They went back a very long way, and Freddie was shattered at Ben's death.

Rightly or wrongly, the Wellington Test match continued to go ahead and petered out in a draw, but not before Freddie had raced to a 33-ball half-century; only Ian Botham had (twice) hit a Test 50 for England in fewer balls. Freddie powered on to make 75, but his muted acknowledgement of the applause for his quickfire 50 showed that his mind was elsewhere and that the achievement was nothing in the context of a young cricketer's tragic loss of life.

Understandably, England's game faltered on that New Zealand tour after Ben's death was announced, and yet the statistics show that Freddie returned home with an average in the Test series of over forty and with a best One-Day International bowling return of 4 for 17 against New Zealand at Auckland.

CHAPTER 8

Prospects of Play Uncertain

'A lot has been said about Freddie's recovery, but you're not talking about a young whippet playing football; this is a sixteen-stone guy trying to bowl fast. It's a totally different stress on the body'

NEIL FAIRBROTHER

There can hardly be a less fortunate way for a young cricketer to end his season than by bagging a pair in a Test match, achingly bowling 27 overs in the same game when clearly unfit and then having to put the bat in temporary storage to undergo a double-hernia operation. But such was Freddie's fate in late August of 2002 and, when he emerged from surgery in September, he cannot for one moment have envisaged that his recovery process would lead to an extraordinary war of words, scupper plans for a family Christmas in Australia, rob him of his chance to play in an Ashes series Down Under, erode his confidence and make him wonder whether or not he still had a future with England at all.

Perhaps, if Freddie hadn't been so willing to put himself

through the pain barrier, if the England management had been a good deal more considerate and sensitive to the injury he was carrying and if England hadn't been so desperate to win the home Test series against India that summer, the furore that engulfed him in the weeks and months that followed his operation might never have arisen.

Freddie was far from fit by the time the selectors got around to naming their team for the Third Test at Headingley against India, when England were one up in the four-Test series after two matches. He had been experiencing pain in his groin for a couple of months, and a hernia operation looked to be the most likely solution. In the long term, with a view to Freddie being fit for the forthcoming tour of Australia, the best thing would have been for Freddie to have missed the Third Test against India and undergo surgery straight away, but the fact was that Andrew Flintoff, as a centrally contracted player, was effectively in the hands of the England management, and they had the final say as to whether he should play at Headingley or not. They decided that he should, although England captain Nasser Hussain later conceded that he probably shouldn't have done so.

In the event, England lost that Third Test by a demoralising innings and 46 runs after Dravid, Tendulkar and Ganguly all scored big 100s as India notched up 628 for 6 (declared). During the innings, Freddie toiled away for 27 overs, which brought his total number of overs bowled in the three Tests to 112, many of them delivered in considerable discomfort. The double-hernia operation that had been beckoning for some while could be delayed no longer.

Once he had come safely through the operation, medical opinion suggested that Freddie ought to be fit in time for the Ashes Tests. Comparisons were made with footballers who had undergone similar operations and the benchmark recovery period appeared to be around eight to ten weeks. It was assumed that Freddie's return to action would fall within a similar time frame, and he was duly picked for the England Ashes squad seemingly without having to prove his fitness in advance. His recuperation and rehabilitation, it was decided, would take place at the National Sports Centre at Lilleshall, and it was felt that his condition would keep improving while he was out in Australia.

But, to the shock and dismay of coach Duncan Fletcher, when Freddie arrived in Perth on 18 October he admitted that he was still unable to run. The England management were aghast – they'd imagined that Freddie should by then have been fit and champing at the bit, ready to take on the Aussies in the First Test in Brisbane on 7 November.

With Darren Gough also breaking down, causing him to be sent home before the First Test without bowling a ball, Flintoff's unavailability due to slow recovery wasn't the news Fletcher wanted. The coach's woes were compounded when Simon Jones suffered terrible cruciate damage in his knee on the opening day of the Test series. As England's injury list continued to grow, it was felt that Freddie might not get the medical attention he needed if he stayed with the squad. The answer, it was decided, was to send him off to the Academy in Adelaide in an effort to speed up his recovery. Freddie worked hard but, when he rejoined the squad and was put through his paces in a pre-Test game against Queensland, it soon became obvious that he wasn't going to be fit for a five-day Test.

Depressingly for Freddie, as the weeks went by there appeared to be no obvious sign of lasting improvement, despite the hard work he was putting in, while the medical experts seemed as bemused by his slow recovery as everyone else. In Australia, Freddie willingly underwent X-rays, an MRI scan and a bone scan in an attempt to get to the root of the problem, and yet nothing untoward showed up.

Disappointingly for the management, deadlines set for his return regularly came and went with no significant progress. His position was reviewed from Test to Test, and once he'd been ruled out of the Second and Third Tests in Adelaide and Perth, respectively, it came down to a question of whether or not he'd make the One-Day Internationals. He did get to play in three warm-up matches, and spent his twenty-fifth birthday still wondering if he would play a part, but, when he was excluded from the official photograph, he knew that his tour was effectively over. The management's patience had grown ever thinner until Duncan Fletcher finally decided that it would be best for all concerned if Freddie returned home for more treatment. The all-rounder's 'will he?'/'won't he?' fitness issues were becoming a distraction to the coach and to team planning. 'Andrew's making no progress at the moment,' said Fletcher. 'He's been checked over in Australia, and everyone over here can't really find a problem, but at this stage he's not fit to play in One-Day Internationals or Test matches and we want him to go and get fit.'

Freddie explained to the media that when he started off bowling he felt comfortable enough, but by the time he was into his third or fourth over he started to feel a bit of pain around his groin area. 'Then it becomes a bit of a struggle in the field as well,' he said, 'and it's difficult, coming back to bowl for second and third spells. If I can go home, see the medical officer and do whatever he says, I'm hoping I can be 100 per cent fit for the World Cup.

'Missing out on the cricket being played out here in the Test matches, and now the One-Day games, is a massive blow and obviously very frustrating. But there's something not quite right with me at the moment and I need to go back and get that sorted out.'

It was a bitterly disappointed Freddie who packed his bags on 12 December for a long flight back to England. And yet, in a way, he was relieved. Being part of an Ashes squad without being able to play was anything but fun, and it was probably better for him to distance himself from it altogether. 'I'm not a good watcher of sports,' he's admitted. 'I can't stand watching football, and I'm not that much better with cricket. If I'm not playing, I'd rather go shopping instead of hanging around, wishing I was part of it all and knowing that I'm not.'

Freddie was the fifth player to return home since the tour began, following Gough, Jones, Ashley Giles (who'd suffered a wrist fracture while practising in the nets) and Chris Silverwood, Jones's replacement, who suffered ligament damage in his ankles. Compounded by Australia's marked superiority in the Tests, it was a sorry tale of woe.

It's possible that Freddie might have flown home and quietly got on with his recuperation with the minimum of fuss if Lord MacLaurin of Knebworth, the outgoing chairman of the ECB, hadn't chosen to speak out. At a point when things could hardly have been worse for Freddie, Lord MacLaurin – in effect, Freddie's ultimate cricket boss – told the media that Freddie hadn't been taking his recuperation from his operation seriously enough and was largely to blame for his own lack of fitness. Not only that but Lord MacLaurin also later repeated his accusations of laziness against Flintoff by stating, 'I had plenty of evidence to say that maybe Freddie didn't do as much as he should have done. Well, he didn't. We know that.' Significantly, however, no official complaint was lodged against Freddie.

Darren Gough, who had been fighting his own fitness battle alongside Freddie at Lilleshall and had seen his efforts towards recuperation at first hand, was furious at this attack on his colleague and immediately leaped to his defence. Lord MacLaurin retorted in an interview, 'It doesn't do any good when Darren Gough comes in and doesn't know what he's talking about.'

By the time a disconsolate Freddie returned to England, controversy was inevitably raging over MacLaurin's remarks. Arriving back on Friday, 13 December, Freddie defiantly rejected MacLaurin's claim. 'There was no foundation to that story,' he told *Sky News*. 'I did my rehab right. It's just unfortunate that I'm still not fit. It's very frustrating for me, and I've just got to get to the bottom of it.'

Duncan Fletcher backed Freddie, saying, 'I've got to take the man at his word. If he says he followed the programme, he did the work.'

The damage, however, had been done. Lord MacLaurin's accusations prompted speculation that Freddie had lapsed back into lazy, undisciplined habits and that he didn't care enough about his game or playing for England. Despite Freddie's denials that he'd been soft-pedalling, Lord MacLaurin's remarks inevitably eroded some of the goodwill and trust that Freddie had built up with the England management. It was a confusing and frustrating time for him, especially as he'd lost the opportunity to fulfil a much-cherished ambition of playing for England in Australia in an Ashes battle.

Quite apart from the natural parental concern that they felt for their son's wellbeing, Freddie's mother and father had other reasons for being upset at his having to abandon the Australia tour: it threw into disarray Colin and Susan Flintoff's carefully laid plans for a family Christmas Down Under. Freddie's parents were set to fly out to Australia in mid-December, in the hope of watching Freddie in action in the Fourth and Fifth Tests, and the plan was for them all to meet up with their other son, Chris, who was due to fly in with his girlfriend from Japan. Because of the continuing question mark hanging over the matter of Freddie's fitness, they'd delayed their decision to travel for as long as possible but had eventually booked a ticket for a three-week supporters' trip that cost them £10,000. Now Freddie was back home and due to embark on an intensive fitness course in England in a race against the 31 December deadline set by the International Cricket Council for the announcement of the squad for the 2003 World Cup.

'It's put a real dampener on things,' said Susan. 'His brother is upset about it. He only comes home once a year and hasn't seen Andrew since last Christmas, and probably won't see him until next Christmas. If it had just been me and Colin, we probably wouldn't have bothered, but with Christopher having made all the arrangements, we'll have to [go].'

It was cruel luck on the family, especially as Colin and Susan had experienced similar disappointment when they travelled to South Africa in 2000 only to see Freddie hobble out of the tour with a stress fracture in his foot. On that occasion, he'd been immediately sent back to England and was home before they were. Now, with Freddie back from Australia, there was nothing for it but to continue with their trip and make the most of it.

As Colin and Susan Flintoff flew out, the war of words about Freddie's attitude continued. On 18 December, Freddie met up with officials from the England and Wales Cricket Board in Birmingham for the first time since arriving back from the tour to thrash out their differences and sort out a regime that would ensure he was fit for the World Cup. This was fast becoming a race against time, since International Cricket Council rules decreed that World Cup teams had to be named by 31 December.

Throughout all the fuss, Flintoff's personal management team, Lancashire's officials and his county teammates had stood loyally behind him. 'I know him very well and how committed he is to getting fit and playing for England,' said Warren Hegg, Flintoff's Lancashire captain, 'so what was said about him was grossly out of order.'

Freddie's personal management were not pleased in the first instance that Freddie seemed pressured into playing against India in the Third Test when it was clearly arguable that it was not in his best interests to do so, delaying his operation and thus robbing him of precious time in which to recover sooner rather than later. Freddie's manager, Andrew 'Chubby' Chandler, was quoted in the *Lancashire Evening Post* as saying, 'The way Andrew has been treated this year has hit him hard. I'm worried that he'll end up not wanting to play again, like he did a couple of years ago.' Some were also of the opinion that Freddie had been inadequately supervised at Lilleshall after his operation.

What perhaps had not been taken sufficiently into account was the fact that a hernia was a serious injury. Not so long ago, a hernia operation might have signalled the end of a footballer's career. And, while great advances had been made in the treatment of sports injuries in recent years, recovery from a hernia op was still something that needed time. Freddie's condition, moreover, was a double hernia, and he wasn't a footballer. Neil Fairbrother hit the nail on the head when he pointed out, 'A lot has been said about Freddie's recovery, but you're not talking about a young whippet playing football. This is a sixteen-stone guy trying to bowl fast. It's a totally different stress on the body.'

Further vindication for Freddie came from Dr Peter Gregory, who had been appointed England's new medical officer on 23 November. After Gregory's first examination, he observed that Freddie had made an unexpectedly slow recovery that was still incomplete, despite undertaking recuperative regimes that were typically carried out by other sportsmen rehabilitating from such surgery. He added, 'He has done all that has been asked of him, in terms of rehabilitation, and we have found no specific reason for the slowness of recovery.'

The meeting in Birmingham between ECB officials, Freddie and Lancashire officials – who were also keen to find out what had gone wrong – helped to clear the air. The upshot was that Freddie would work hard with Lancashire physio Dave Roberts and under the eye of Dr Gregory in the hope that he could pass the fitness tests in time to be named for the World Cup.

Up to Christmas and beyond, Freddie spent up to six hours a day engaged in training routines that involved cycling, running around the hills in Bolton and gym exercises geared to strengthening his abdomen and back. There were also varying spells of bowling to judge how many overs he could cope with before suffering groin trouble. By the time the Lancashire players arrived for pre-season training, Freddie was able to prove in tests that he was the second fittest of the lot. He was also passed as fit for the World Cup, and was even able to return to Australia on 17 January 2003 in time to play against the Aussies for the first time in Melbourne, in the second final of the VB series – a day–night game – on 25 January. In that game, Australia won by 5 runs and Freddie reached 16 before being bowled by Man Of The Match Brett Lee. On that occasion, Freddie's 10 overs went for 56, but he did have the pleasure of taking his first Aussie wicket, and it was a big one: Adam Gilchrist for 26, just when he was starting to look dangerous.

Things were definitely looking up for Andrew Flintoff, and 2003 was going to be a very special year.

CHAPTER 9

Lording it at HQ

'Come on, Flintoff. Come on. Be the cricketer you can be.'

MARK NICHOLAS'S EXHORTATION WHILE COMMENTATING FOR CHANNEL 4 ON THE SECOND TEST BETWEEN ENGLAND AND SOUTH AFRICA AT LORD'S, 2003

In the fascinating cricketing treasure house at Lord's that is the MCC Museum, there lies on the second floor, safely encased behind glass, a Woodworm Premier Wand cricket bat lying on its side. Running down the middle, from the shoulder of the bat to the toe of the blade, is a large crack in the wood that all but divides the blade into two. ON LOAN FROM A. FLINTOFF, reads a neatly printed inscription beneath this shattered relic of an epic encounter between willow and leather. Beside it are two photographs of Freddie in action with this particular bat during the Test against South Africa at Lord's in 2003.

The first photograph shows him thumping a ball to midwicket, while the second shows him holding his shattered bat aloft and another small inscription informs visitors to the museum that this was the bat that Freddie broke while making 142 in the second innings of the match. As a lasting piece of evidence of a Test-match innings that was smashing in every sense, this slice of wrecked willow well merits its place in such a hallowed location, but it doesn't begin to tell anything like the whole extraordinary, thrilling story.

It's an obvious and trite observation but, as any cricketer who has ever trod the turf at St John's Wood will testify, playing at Lord's is something never to be forgotten. A selection of hoardings posted prominently at various points around the ground remind spectators just what a momentous privilege it is.

'Walking through the Long Room past all the members and on to the turf gave you goosepimples. It was a fantastic feeling,' is Allan Lamb's testimony on a hoarding attached to the back of the Allen Stand on the right of the pavilion.

'Lord's is a very special place for all cricketers to play,' Michael Vaughan is quoted as saying on the hoarding at the back of the Tavern Stand. 'At Lord's there's a buzz about the place, whether you're playing a county game or a big international.'

It goes without saying that to play for one's country at the headquarters of cricket is one of the most cherished ambitions of any cricketer. To achieve that aim is a treasured moment for any player. To score a century in a Test match at Lord's is the stuff of dreams for all but a few. Andrew Strauss managed it on his first attempt, but many a top-quality international batsman has played wonderfully in more than one Test match at Lord's and yet has never achieved that distinction.

Others, maybe less gifted, have surpassed themselves to reach three figures, inspired perhaps to rise to the occasion by walking the dozen or so steps through the famous Long Room that leads them out on to the field. On the way through, they will have passed an awe-inspiring collection of cricketing art and memorabilia, including portraits of Thomas Lord, Sir Donald Bradman, Sir Leonard Hutton and Douglas Jardine, the architect of the infamous 'bodyline' bowling that caused so much controversy in the 1930s.

It is reaching the magic three-figure score and, similarly, the feat of taking five wickets in an innings that earn players the right to have their names added to the Lord's honours boards, attached to the walls of the dressing rooms on the second floor of the 'Cathedral of Cricket', as the pavilion is known.

Players entering the home dressing room, situated in the south tower of the pavilion – the one nearest the Grace Gates – are greeted by an honours board for England Test-match centurions dating back to 1884. This display lists the initials and surname of each centurion, along with the date on which his 100 was achieved, his total score and the country that served as opposition. A matching board, which also dates back to a first instance in 1884, lists England bowlers who finished with a 5-wicket haul. Similar honours boards adorn the walls of the visitors' dressing room, registering comparable feats accomplished by tourists in Tests at the home of cricket.

While these honours boards are a reminder in indelible black ink of famous past deeds, failure at Lord's can leave its own lasting, intensely personal mark upon a player. Every single cricketer who has ever stepped on to the ground's playing surface has been desperate to do well at Lord's, which is why failure there is all the more disappointing, and somehow magnified by the rich heritage and sheer aura surrounding the world's most famous cricket ground.

As Tom Graveney, that most elegant and modest of England batsmen in the 1950s, once wrote, 'To fail at Lord's seems to be a personal matter, and the sight of those silent, illustrious members looking the other way as you pass through their ranks leaves no doubt as to their feelings.' Graveney, it must be said, usually made plenty of runs when he played for England at Lord's. The solitary Test duck recorded in the Lord's scorebooks against his name came against the West Indies in 1957 and was his only significant failure at the ground in Tests – which is perhaps why he felt the silence of the Long Room so keenly as he made his way back to the dressing room. Normally he returned with applause ringing in his ears.

It says much about Andrew Flintoff that, in the space of four days at Lord's, in the summer of 2003, after first experiencing a failure with the bat at Lord's that was deemed foolish and irresponsible by most of the spectators, by the press, by TV commentators and by the ranks of watching MCC members in the pavilion, he roused himself to return to the crease second time around to play an innings that will live long in the memory of those lucky enough to have witnessed it.

On Thursday, 31 July, he had been admonished on television in the most disparaging fashion by Mike Atherton for playing 'brainless cricket'. By the end of Sunday, 3 August, Freddie was being given a standing ovation by a packed crowd all the way back to the pavilion for playing one of the most sparkling innings by a number seven ever seen in a Test at Lord's.

It was some transformation, and very definitely a turning point in the international career of Andrew Flintoff. It was a turning point for the England team, too; Freddie's innings offered them hope and something very positive to take away from the game in what was a severe drubbing for England. Freddie's performance on that occasion went some way to stemming the tide and checking the momentum that South Africa had built up in the first two Tests of the series.

To appreciate in every way Freddie's heroics in what was a crucial Test Match, one has to consider events of just three days earlier, when England cricket suffered unexpected upheaval with the sudden resignation of Nasser Hussain as Test captain.

The South Africans had arrived in England ranked second in the world under the captaincy of Graeme Smith, a confident young man who at that time was just twenty-two and one of the youngest-ever skippers on his first major tour.

Hussain, in contrast, had been under pressure for some time, particularly since Michael Vaughan had taken over after the World Cup as skipper of the England One-Day side and was earning glowing plaudits for his captaincy in the press. Vaughan quickly proved to be a successful captain in England's limited-overs game, and to many observers – not least Hussain – there appeared to be a new vibrancy among the players under Vaughan's leadership.

Hussain had also noticed how much the players seemed to be enjoying playing under Vaughan in the One-Day Internationals, and when he arrived at Edgbaston for the First Test against South Africa he sensed that things had changed in the England dressing room: it was no longer his team. As the game wore on, Hussain became more and more convinced that it was time to pass the baton to the younger man.

A record opening partnership of 338 between Smith and Gibbs, the former going on to make 277 in a total of 594, did nothing to change Hussain's mind that it was time to step down. On that occasion, Freddie made a competent 40 to help England save the follow-on, and as soon as the match was drawn Hussain announced his tenure of the captaincy was over. This left Michael Vaughan just two rest days to pick up the reins before the start of the Lord's Test, just forty-eight hours in which to gather his thoughts, marshal his troops as captain and formulate his own ideas and strategy.

Soon after being installed as captain, Vaughan had dinner

with Michael Atherton, who urged him to make Freddie the fulcrum of his side, the pivotal man around whom the team could revolve. With Darren Gough – for so long the team's talisman – contemplating retirement from Test cricket, Freddie was his obvious successor. It wasn't just Freddie's ability with bat and ball that made him the main man, the central figure; in Atherton's experience, Freddie had a natural way of drawing people around him. As a batsman, Atherton had always been an excellent timer of the ball, and his assessment of Freddie's role in his conversation with Vaughan was made with similar perfect Atherton timing.

Freddie, for his part, was at last showing signs that he could shoulder the kind of responsibility Atherton had in mind, having begun the season playing well for Lancashire and making important contributions for England in the One-Day Internationals that made him an automatic selection for the Tests. In the limited-overs games against South Africa, he had made an impact as batsman, bowler and fielder. He then went on to make a whirlwind 32, not out, at the Oval and showed Makhaya Ntini that he had the skill, courage and panache to hook the fast bowler off his nose for a six that soared in the general direction of the gasometer. He took vital wickets and, in plunging full length to his right to take a sensational catch to get rid of Jacques Kallis at Edgbaston, he displayed a streak of brilliance of the kind that will always lift a team.

By the time he came to Lord's for the Second Test, Freddie had every right to feel pleased with the way things were going.

His form was generally good and he felt in good nick. Earlier in the season, he had lit up Lord's with a spectacular run-a-ball innings of 111 against Middlesex in the County Championship. That century – his tenth – included two changes of bat and four sixes.

Freddie also harboured some happy recent memories of the same ground, having some three weeks earlier taken two top wickets, and he had been batting at the end of the match when England crushed South Africa by 7 wickets in the final of the NatWest triangular series. The one-sided match was all over remarkably quickly, leaving Freddie and the other England players lingering long in the dressing room, savouring their victory while a despondent Graeme Smith gathered his players around him on the Lord's outfield and told them to remember the hurt of this thrashing when they returned to Lord's to take on England again in the Test match in a few weeks' time.

In the First Test match against the South Africans at Edgbaston, Freddie felt that he'd been batting well enough, and might have gone on to a big score if he hadn't been undone by a ball that kept unusually low. He hadn't played Test-match cricket for a year, but now that he was very much back in the England set-up he was beginning to feel that he was rightfully there and could have an influence in the outcome of a game. He felt comfortable in the side and more assured of his role, and has admitted on several occasions that, on his return to the England fold that summer, he'd felt as though he'd finally had the chance to draw a line under everything that had gone before.

And England needed an Andrew Flintoff buoyed with confidence and self-belief if they were to compete hard with the South Africans. The tourists were a formidable unit, comprising a blend of brilliance from opening batsman, Herschelle Gibbs; grit from Gary Kirsten, batting number three; prodigious run-getting and excellent seam bowling from Jacques Kallis; a top wicketkeeper-batsman in Mark Boucher; and an opening attack of Shaun Pollock and Allan Donald that could be devastating. The First Test had shown that they batted a long way down and were going to be very hard to beat.

At Lord's, Vaughan's reign as captain got off to the worst possible start. He lost the toss and, on what seemed a decent strip, England were bundled out on the first day for 173. There were audible groans from the crowd as first Vaughan and then Stewart got out, caught after hooking, and Freddie came to the wicket with England tottering precariously on 85 for 5. After two leading batsman had largely contributed to their own downfall by injudiciously playing the hook shot, it was down to Freddie to knuckle down and play a disciplined innings to get England out of deep trouble – more especially so when the score slumped to 112 for 7. Instead, he too got out after hooking.

Freddie had progressed untroubled to 11 when South Africa's quickest bowler, Makhaya Ntini, tempted Freddie with a shortish ball. The invitation to hook was irresistible but, as he went through with the shot, Ntini's excited cry of 'Catch it!' must have told him he had fallen straight into a trap. Perfectly positioned on the square-leg boundary precisely for such a shot was Paul Adams, who barely had to move from his fielding position in front of the Grand Stand in order to take a straightforward catch. Ntini whooped with delight as a despondent-looking Freddie turned and headed slowly back to the pavilion.

Around the ground, there was a general sense of dismay from the spectators mixed with murmurs of disapproval at the way Freddie had got out. He had been suckered out – it was as simple as that. He had gone for the hook when England were looking for him to be more circumspect and build an innings. The murmurs from the crowd increased in volume as Freddie's indiscretion was replayed painfully for the spectators on the giant screen above the Edrich Stand at the Nursery End of the ground. In households and pubs around England, cricket fans watching the action and then several replays on their screens heard Atherton's scathing reaction to Freddie's dismissal: 'It's brainless cricket. It really is. The number of times we've seen Andrew Flintoff pick out the man at deep square leg this summer. Once again, Andrew Flintoff has played some brainless cricket.' Channel 4's chief cricket presenter, Mark Nicholas, was no less severe on Freddie, commenting caustically, 'It's a shocker, frankly.'

On that first day of the Test, I was just one of a host of

MCC members watching play at Lord's and, therefore, Freddie's dismissal from the pavilion's Long Room. Around me, distinguished-looking gentlemen sporting their distinctive bacon-and-egg, orange-and-yellow MCC ties were muttering, 'Stupid, just stupid,' and shaking their heads in irritation with Freddie for holing out in such a manner.

Ian Botham famously discovered what an unforgiving place the Lord's pavilion can be when he walked back up the stone steps after completing a pair by getting bowled around his legs by Ray Bright against Australia in 1981. Now Freddie, too, found that MCC members can be icily judgemental. Back in 1981, Botham had disappeared back into the pavilion in silence, the members turning away in embarrassment or burying their heads in their copies of *The Times* as he passed by on his way back to the dressing room. After a fruitless year as captain and a personally disappointing match, Botham recognised from the reaction of the members that he was no longer deemed the man suitable to captain England and resigned almost immediately afterwards.

Freddie was given much the same disdainful treatment by the MCC members as he walked up the steps into the Long Room, took a left turn for a few more uncomfortable paces and then turned right at the end of the Long Room, through the door, to mount the flight of stairs that led back up to the England dressing room.

Tom Graveney had succinctly summed up the atmosphere that surrounds a player after failure at Lord's, and now Freddie too experienced similar treatment as he passed through the massed ranks in the pavilion, with 'illustrious members looking the other way leaving no doubt as to their feelings'.

To complete a miserable first day for England at the showpiece Lord's Test, Hussain dropped Graeme Smith – the double centurion of the First Test – when the South African captain had made just 8. The catch was a sitter, hit straight to him at cover at comfortable height, and he spilled it. Unfortunately for Hussain and England, Smith went on batting for another nine hours to make 259 as South Africa scored a massive 682 before declaring.

Freddie was the pick of the bowlers and toiled away manfully and economically, but he had the misfortune to have two catches dropped off his bowling during this run glut, during which he sent down no less than 40 overs – 18 more than Steve Harmison and 12 more than Darren Gough. Significantly, on a pitch offering little help to the bowlers, Freddie had been the workhorse for Vaughan in his first Test match as captain. It was a role to which he would have to become accustomed in the next couple of years.

Trailing by the massive margin of 509, England were staring right down the barrel of a very heavy defeat. It would need a monumental effort, a miracle, persistent rain or even all three to save them. With the weather increasingly set at 'fair', the odds were stacked against them, but the wicket remained good and they were determined to bat well and at least put down a few markers for the Tests to come. By the close on the third day, England were 129 for 2, and a big crowd turned up on the following day, the Sunday, expecting an England defeat but hoping at least to see a dogged rearguard action. Those who decided that the match was as good as over and stayed away were to miss a real treat.

All of England's top order got a start without going on to make a really big score, and England were indeed sliding inexorably to miserable defeat when Freddie came out to bat with the score on 208 for 5. This rapidly became 208 for 6, leaving Freddie to bat with just the tail. The stark facts were that England were still more than 300 runs behind with just 4 wickets left and the weather unchanged – fine and sunny; rain was never going to be a factor in helping to save England that day. A South African victory was inevitable, and Freddie knew that he had nothing to lose by going for his shots, as long as he didn't do anything too silly.

While Ashley Giles gave good support at the other end, Freddie settled in and began to take the fight to the South African fast bowlers. He needed a bit of luck, especially when he played almost a carbon copy of the hook shot that had got him out in the first innings, but this time the ball fell short of a fielder, prompting TV commentator Dermott Reeve to chide, 'Well, would you credit it! Nearly an action replay of his first-innings dismissal – same bowler, same shot – and there's a man back there. Andrew Flintoff needs to programme his brain.'

Reeve was soon changing his tune. Flintoff's cricket brain

was programmed, all right; it was switched to 'Play your natural game.' Growing in confidence and riding his luck, Freddie began to find the boundary with a series of flowing, powerful strokes, and soon the partisan crowd were revelling in Freddie's show of defiance and loudly cheering every mighty swing of his bat. On the terraces, between overs, dozens of mobile phones were suddenly activated to relay messages to friends, urging them to turn on the TV at once as something fairly spectacular was starting to unfold at Lord's. England might be going down to a comprehensive defeat, but Flintoff was going down with all guns blazing.

Freddie's confrontation with Ntini, who bowled very fast from the Pavilion End, was a thrilling duel. The South African did him for sheer pace on a couple of occasions, then found himself impudently whacked high over the square-leg boundary into the crowd in the Tavern Stand. Twice Ntini hit Freddie on the helmet as the batsman tried to sway out of line in resisting the temptation to hook, not wishing to repeat the mistake of the first innings. If Freddie was ruffled by the blows on the head, he didn't show it and came up smiling both times. His response was just to get on with it and, later, to hit four Ntini deliveries in succession to the boundary.

There then came a marvellous moment that summed up the duel. Aiming for another big hit from a quick delivery, Freddie's bat shattered and split in two, right down the middle. Ntini instinctively raised both arms above his head, claiming at least a moral victory, but Freddie swiftly regained the initiative with a defiant signal to the dressing room for a replacement. He held the shattered blade aloft in a wooden V-for-victory sign. His bat might have been broken, but he was unbowed.

This passage of play contained some thrilling cricket, and Freddie's teammates all gathered on the England balcony to applaud the fours and sixes that were starting to come with increasing regularity. Freddie's aggressive tactics clearly got under the skin of South African captain Graeme Smith, standing at slip. Rattled, and frustrated at how the South African victory charge was being held up, Smith had plenty to say to Freddie.

A straight drive for four off Pretorius brought Freddie to his 50, and he had taken his score into the 80s when he was joined by Steve Harmison, coming in at number ten. On a gloriously sunny afternoon with not a hope of rain coming to England's aid, the big fast bowler's only thought was to stay there to see his great friend through to his first Test century in England, and he set about giving Freddie as much of the strike as possible. Harmison duly managed to keep his wicket intact long enough for Freddie to reach his 100 with a controlled pull for four off Ntini. His century was rapturously received by the crowd, his teammates and the MCC members in the pavilion, many of whom were the very same gentlemen who had barely cast him a glance after his 'brainless' dismissal three days earlier.

Freddie had at last delivered the kind of Test innings on

home soil that English cricket fans had long believed he was capable of but had begun to despair he would ever produce. It was his second Test century, but Freddie's own reaction to reaching the milestone was notably muted. His acknowledgement was barely cursory. He realised all too well that he was playing his innings in a losing cause and that it would have absolutely no bearing on the result of the match. He knew it, and the South Africans knew it. And so did the spectators, who included his fiancée, Rachael. But that didn't detract from his achievement, nor from the entertainment, and it didn't stop the excited crowd from cheering Freddie's wonderful exhibition of big-hitting.

Having reached his 100, Freddie played with ever-greater freedom. Wrist spinner Paul Adams was slammed for six into the sight screen at the Nursery End, medium pacer Andrew Hall was belted for another big six over long on, and one extraordinary over from Shaun Pollock had the crowd repeatedly rising to their feet as Freddie launched a pugnacious attack on a bowler who is normally a miser when it comes to giving the batsmen scoring deliveries.

First, Freddie drove Pollock straight back over his head for a magnificent six into the crowd at the Nursery End, and then he followed up with two drives of brutal power that raced through the covers and over the rope in front of the Mound Stand for four. When Pollock adjusted his line and bowled wider, Freddie was up on his toes to carve another powerful four through the off side, this time past backward point. In all, he took 20 off that one Pollock over, scoring 6–4–4–4–2 off consecutive balls and earned a standing ovation from the 25,000-strong crowd at the end of it. No one could remember the last time – if ever – Pollock had been treated in such a manner in a Test match.

Freddie had passed his previous Test best of 137, made in New Zealand, and had chalked up 142 from 146 balls, with eighteen fours and five huge sixes, when he was finally stumped off Adams down the leg side while going for another big hit. He was the last man out, and the game was lost, but it had been an electrifying innings and the entire ground rose as one to applaud him every step of his way back to the pavilion. This time, his path back up the pavilion steps was lined by MCC members who had risen to their feet in unison to applaud him, and there was even the odd pat on the back for Freddie as he moved through the Long Room.

The bald facts were that England had lost the match by an innings and 72 runs. It was a crushing defeat, and Ntini became the first South African bowler to take 10 wickets in a Lord's Test, while Smith's score of 259 beat by 5 runs Sir Donald Bradman's seventy-three-year record for an overseas player in a Lord's Test. However, the final day is remembered for Freddie's 142, the highest score by a number seven in a Lord's Test, beating the 137 by England's wicketkeeper-batsman Les Ames scored way back in 1931. The name 'Andrew Flintoff' was duly added to the honours board in the England dressing room.

Freddie's ton earned him the distinction of joining a select band of Lord's Test centurions who include some of England's greatest-ever batsmen, among them Jack Hobbs, Frank Woolley, Wally Hammond, Len Hutton, Denis Compton and Peter May. To be bracketed in such illustrious company was indeed an honour. Thumbing through the record books, statisticians noted that Freddie's Bothamesque innings took place almost exactly twenty years after Beefy had made his only Test 100 at Lord's, against Pakistan. And, as a lasting reminder of a memorable innings, Freddie's shattered Woodworm bat was found a special place in a glass case in the Lord's Museum, situated behind the pavilion.

'It was due to go as I'd been using it for quite a while,' said Freddie with a rueful smile after the game as he surveyed the remnants of the broken blade. But there was no trace of elation when asked about his innings. He said he was just trying to get good partnerships going and regretted that his knock didn't influence the outcome of the match. 'It was too little, too late.'

Michael Vaughan, who had conspicuously led the applause for Freddie from the England balcony for his 100, felt that Freddie's ton could be a major turning point in his international career. 'When any player plays a big Test innings, it gives them immense confidence,' he enthused, 'and the way that he played, the opposition he was up against and being in front of a full house at Lord's will give him a huge confidence boost going into the next game, and hopefully for the future. I thought Freddie was outstanding with the ball on Saturday but without any luck, and he actually told me that night he wanted to have a bet to see if he could get 100, but I told him we weren't allowed. He was pretty confident. I hope it will be a breakthrough innings for him, because he's a real asset to this team. He's such a powerful man that all he's got to do is choose the right ball to hit.'

Vaughan was hopeful that Freddie would go on from this 100 to be more consistent at Test level than he had been after his only previous Test century against New Zealand. 'He got 100 in New Zealand and then he stood still a bit, but hopefully this can really trigger him off into some kind of form and keep him playing the way he has done. He played brilliantly for us in the One-Dayers, and he's started well in the Tests. His shot selection was outstanding and he chose the right ball to hit, which is all he had to do, because he has that many shots and he's so powerful. His defensive shot goes for four, so he generally doesn't need to hit the ball that hard; he can block it for four.'

The sheer brute power that Freddie displayed that day in his strokeplay reminded many of Ian Botham at his best and couldn't help but further the comparison between the two. From England's perspective, Freddie's innings had salvaged some pride for England and saved them from enduring an even more emphatic defeat, and had gone more than a little way towards checking South Africa's superiority in the series

ENGLAND v SOUTH AFRICA

Second npower Test, Lord's, 31 July/1–3 August 2003

ENGLAND	First Innings		Second Innings	
ME Trescothick	b Ntini	**6**	c Adams b Ntini	**23**
***MP Vaughan**	c sub b Ntini	**33**	c Pollock b Hall	**29**
MA Butcher	c Hall b Pollock	**19**	c Kirsten b Hall	**70**
N Hussain	b Hall	**14**	c Boucher b Ntini	**61**
A McGrath	c Kirsten b Hall	**4**	c Boucher b Pollock	**13**
+AJ Stewart	c Adams b Ntini	**7**	c Hall b Ntini	**0**
A Flintoff	c Adams b Ntini	**11**	st Boucher b Adams	**142**
AF Giles	c Pollock b Hall	**7**	c Pollock b Ntini	**23**
D Gough	c Adams b Pollock	**34**	c Adams b Pollock	**14**
SJ Harmison	b Ntini	**0**	c Hall b Ntini	**7**
JM Anderson	not out	**21**	not out	**4**
	Extras	**17**		**31**
	TOTAL	**173**		**417**

FALL OF WICKETS

1/52, 2/60, 3/186, 4/258, 1/11, 2/35, 3/73, 4/77, 5/85, 5/208, 6/208, 7/297, 6/96, 7/109, 8/112, 9/118, 8/344, 9/371, 10/417, 10/173

BOWLING

First Innings		Second Innings	
Pollock	**14.4–5–28–2**	**Pollock**	**29–7–105–2**
Ntini	**17–3–75–5**	**Ntini**	**31–5–145–5**
Pretorius	**4–0–20–0**	**Hall**	**24–6–60–2**
Hall	**10–4–18–3**	**Adams**	**20.1–1–74–1**
Adams	**3–0–19–0**	**Pretorius**	**3–0–16–0**

SOUTH AFRICA

***GC Smith** b Anderson	**259**
HH Gibbs b Harmison	**49**
G Kirsten b McGrath	**108**
HH Dippenaar c Butcher b Giles	**92**
JA Rudolph c Stewart b Flintoff	**26**
+MV Boucher b Anderson	**68**
SM Pollock not out	**10**
AJ Hall not out	**6**
Extras	**64**
TOTAL (6 wkts dec)	**682**

PR Adams, D Pretorius and M Ntini did not bat.

FALL OF WICKETS

1/33, 2/390, 3/513, 4/580, 5/630, 6/672

BOWLING

First Innings

Gough	**28–3–127–0**
Anderson	**27–6–90–2**
Harmison	**22–3–103–1**
Flintoff	**40–10–115–1**
Giles	**43–5–142–1**
Butcher	**6–1–19–0**
McGrath	**11–0–40–1**

UMPIRES

SA Bucknor (West Indies) and DB Hair (Australia).

Third umpire: P Willey. Referee: RS Madugalle (Sri Lanka).

South Africa won by an innings and 92 runs. Toss: South Africa.

thus far. South Africa had won handsomely, and the dominance of bat over ball while compiling their massive total of nearly 700 at Lord's prompted England's Darren Gough to announce his retirement from Test cricket.

With 'Dazzler' Gough and his unquenchable spirit gone from the team, Freddie was now the natural successor as England's talisman. Until that Lord's Test, the South African view of Freddie might have been that he was little more than a dasher, a batsman who invariably gave a bowler a chance by the very nature of the way he played, but after that match there came to be a growing respect for him among the opposition. They knew now precisely how destructive he could be and realised that, in a very different match situation from the one at Lord's, Freddie could be a real danger if allowed to get on top of the bowling. And so it was to prove later in the series.

CHAPTER 10

Man of the Series

'He bestrides the Test field like Beowulf among his retainers, ready to do battle with giants or monsters.'

FORMER ENGLAND CAPTAIN MIKE BREARLEY
ON ANDREW FLINTOFF

By the time the name 'Andrew Flintoff' had been added to the honours board in the England dressing room, Freddie was on his way home with congratulations pouring in from all quarters for his wonderful Lord's knock. His innings was greeted with special pride at St Anne's Cricket Club, where former teammates, coaches and club officials could hardly contain their excitement. Having watched their young protégé dish out similar sort of punishment to bowlers right throughout his teens, it was tempting to say, 'I told you so' to anyone who had doubted that Freddie could cut it at the highest level.

For the selectors, Freddie's performance was one of the few positives that England could take out of the Lord's match. They were still saddled with the task of coming up with a team for the Third Test at Trent Bridge that could bowl out the South Africans twice. And for the bowlers, most pressing of all was finding a way to take Graeme Smith's wicket. Incredibly, Smith had scored 621 runs in just 3 innings in two Tests and professed to be hungry for more. The bowlers were sick of the sight of him.

After his 142 at Lord's, Freddie came down to earth with a bump at Trent Bridge, where he was out for a duck in England's first innings, which totalled 445 thanks to 100s by both Butcher and Hussain. When it was South Africa's turn to bat, Smith still looked in ominously good touch, but, to the enormous relief of the whole England team, Freddie produced a clever and thoughtful piece of bowling to see the back of him for 35.

During his marathon 40-over bowling stint at Lord's, Freddie had noticed that the young South African captain tended to step unusually far back into his crease when playing off the back foot. He pointed this out at a team meeting and suggested that it was well worth trying to push the left-hander further and further back in his crease in the hope that he might hit his wicket. Bowling to plan, Freddie had the rewarding sight of Smith stepping back and treading on his stumps. Freddie was exuberant; his plan had worked like a charm and Smith's departure gave the spirits of the entire team a much-needed boost.

England managed to gain a lead of 83 in their first innings, and with the pitch deteriorating they needed to bat well second time around to press home their advantage. By the time Freddie came out to bat, however, they'd slumped to 44 for 5. The irregular bounce in the wicket suggested that no batsman could expect any sort of permanence, and Freddie rightly figured that the situation required him to play his shots. The pitch threatened to get him out at any time anyway, so, if he collected a few boundaries, those runs would probably turn out to be priceless in setting South Africa a target.

Freddie made a rapid 30 – including one magnificent six, an effortless pivot on his left foot to hoist Kallis over long on – which proved to be joint top score in England's total of 118 and, in a tight game, did indeed prove invaluable. When South Africa began to chase 202 for victory, they were soon in trouble and James Kirtley – with the help of a pitch that increasingly misbehaved – wrapped up victory for England on the fifth day by taking 6 for 34. Michael Vaughan's winning of the toss had been vital and England had enjoyed much the best of the conditions. The series was now level at one all.

The teams barely had time to pause for breath before it was on to Headingley, Leeds, for the Fourth Test three days later. Yorkshire cricket fans have traditionally reserved their own special kind of welcome for Lancastrians in the Battles of the Roses, and Freddie, like any Lancastrian, has always been especially keen to give a good account of himself at Headingley. Now, wearing England's three lions instead of Lancashire's red rose, he would be glad just to score even a single run at the ground.

In Freddie's previous four Tests at Leeds, he'd been out for a duck each time and lasted less than a dozen balls in total. Happily for him, a half-century in each innings now helped him to put his Headingley nightmares behind him, while 2 wickets in each innings made his an impressive individual bowling performance. But it wasn't enough in a match that England somehow contrived to lose after having had the South Africans reeling at 21 for 4 on the first morning.

Thanks to Kirsten digging in with a determined 130, South Africa recovered and Kallis took 6 for 54 in England's second innings to send them tumbling to a crushing defeat by 191 runs. They'd managed it, too, without the services of Shaun Pollock, who had flown home to attend the birth of his first child. The South Africans' momentum was back and they moved on to the Oval needing just a draw to clinch their first Test-series victory in England since 1965.

The extraordinary, fluctuating drama that unfolded at the Fifth Test between England and South Africa in early September 2003 must rank among the best-ever matches played at south-east London's Oval Cricket Ground. Over five of the most fascinating days of cricket imaginable, capacity crowds watched England accomplish a remarkable and highly improbable reversal of their fortunes to rescue a cause that was seemingly hopelessly lost on the first day.

This game had everything, and then some. In the glorious certainty of hindsight, all sorts of ingredients contributed to a thrilling mix: an exhilarating first double 100 by Marcus

Trescothick; an astonishing comeback full of character from Graham Thorpe, whose previous 3 innings against South Africa had all been ducks; an emotional final hurrah from Alec Stewart, emerging through a generous South African guard of honour to end an illustrious Test career on his home ground; and a timely performance from veteran bowler Martin Bicknell reminding everyone what might have been if the selectors hadn't repeatedly overlooked him for so long.

All of this made for a potent cricketing feast, and that's before one takes into consideration a stylish 183 from South African opener Gibbs, the flukish downfall of Kallis and a breathtaking, match-changing innings from Freddie that made a mockery of a major bookmakers' odds of forty to one against an England victory after the first day's play. Add in the breaking of a Test record that had stood for 111 years and it still doesn't begin to tell the story of an incredible match.

Freddie and the other England bowlers must have groaned when Vaughan lost the toss and South Africa instantly chose to bat on a perfect wicket with a fast outfield. Nearing the end of a sun-drenched first day, South Africa had passed 350 for the loss of just 3 wickets, thanks to a fabulous 100 from Herschelle Gibbs and 90 from a typically imperturbable Gary Kirsten. Then a fourth wicket at the end of the final session gave a glimmer of hope for England and something to cheer for to a full house disgruntled and starting to voice their displeasure at seeing the home side powerless to stop the South African batsmen from batting England out of the game.

By rights, South Africa should have gone on to do just that. England cricket followers gloomily expected the worst on the second day, which began with London bookmakers echoing the gloomiest fears of the fans by posting those odds of forty to one against an England victory. But England clawed their way back into the match, helped by two run-outs, including the crucial wicket of Kallis, a non-striker when Giles deflected the ball on to the stumps with Kallis out of his ground.

At 432 for 9, England were still just about in with a chance if they could wrap up the innings quickly, but South Africa's Shaun Pollock – restored to the side after the birth of his daughter – showed all his experience to engineer the strike and add 52 for the last wicket. With that last partnership, England's chance, it seemed, had gone.

The pessimists could point to the stark reality of the match situation – that England needed to make 285 in order to avoid the follow-on – but a draw for England wouldn't do; they needed a win to level the series. The positive assessment in the England camp was that the wicket was still a belter for batting, but that they would have to make 600 if they were to have any outside chance of victory.

They were 78 for the loss of Michael Vaughan and Mark Butcher when Graham Thorpe – playing international cricket for the first time in fourteen months – joined Marcus Trescothick. Together they put on 268, with Trescothick scoring 219 and Thorpe 124. Alec Stewart then made a sparkling 38 in his last Test innings before departing the Oval to tumultuous cheers every step of the way back to the pavilion.

The shift in the watching spectators' attitude reflected the events on the pitch. As the boundaries flowed, appreciative applause for Trescothick's and Thorpe's prolific partnership and England's brave fightback gradually turned to mounting excitement with the realisation that England had given themselves just a sniff of a chance of winning the game. Freddie came in to bat when the fifth wicket fell, with England just 4 runs behind South Africa's total, and by the end of the third day England had nosed ahead of South Africa's total of 484 by 18 runs, with Freddie having made a circumspect 10, not out. The pitch was still playing perfectly and the smart money was on a draw.

Before start of play on the fourth morning, all the talk in the England camp was still about trying to extend the slender lead with the remaining 3 wickets to reach a total of 600 in order to put South Africa under pressure in their second innings. The responsibility for taking the score up to those heady heights clearly lay with Freddie as the last of the recognised batsmen.

Resuming on 502 for 7, this plan suffered a serious setback when Bicknell was out to the third ball of the day without scoring. His experienced play would have been useful with Freddie up at the other end, and his departure left Freddie with just the two bowlers, Harmison and Anderson, to come, neither of whom professed to know much about the art of batting.

Arriving at the crease, Harmison nevertheless told his great friend that he had no intention of getting out and reminded Freddie that the team needed to push the total up to or as near to 600 as possible.

To his credit, Harmison kept his end up, kept out the bowlers, kept his wicket intact and took 21 balls to get off the mark.

Having batted at number seven for England throughout the series, Freddie had learned quite a bit about batting with the tail. He had also watched the way in which Pollock had gone about doing the same thing for South Africa. Now he managed to farm as much of the strike as he could while taking the attack to the South African fast bowlers.

In a dynamic onslaught that electrified another excited Sunday-morning crowd packed into the Oval, Freddie proceeded to smash 85 more runs with the next 72 balls he faced, putting on a record-breaking 99 for the ninth wicket with Harmison, whose contribution was just 3. The partnership surpassed England's previous ninth-wicket record of 71 against South Africa that had stood since 1891–2.

As he did at Lord's for his innings of 142, Freddie rode his luck, twice seeing attempted big hits drop short of fielders, much to the exasperation of Kallis, the bowler. When Freddie next connected perfectly and smashed Kallis for six over midwicket, the bowler stood with his hands on his hips, staring at him in irritation. He reached 1,000 runs in Test cricket with a flashing drive off Kallis, and got to 50 with a miscue – this time a pull off Ntini that fell safe and earned him 2 runs.

Again, as at Lord's, his big-hitting forced him to change his bat, but this brought no respite for the South African bowlers, while the body language of their fielders told its own story. Freddie was taking the match away from them, and captain Graeme Smith was becoming increasingly rattled. He was to be seen expressing various opinions and character assessments of Freddie from his position at slip, not least when Ntini was forced to trot all the way down to the popping crease to pick up the ball after it dropped at Freddie's feet from a defensive shot. Freddie might have obliged by picking up the ball himself and tossing it back to the bowler or tapping it to a fielder, but not that day. Battle had been well and truly joined, and the message was, 'I'm batting. It's your job to do the fielding.'

Somewhat predictably, Ntini dropped the next ball short, but Freddie was waiting for it and crashed it away towards the gasometer. He was waiting, too, for the next ball, pitched up and, with a clean swing of the bat, hit it straight back over the bowler's head for another six. In all, Ntini went for 31 in 3 overs. It was thrilling batting, and Freddie had the crowd rising to him.

Smith's frontline pace bowlers were taking such a battering that the South African captain felt compelled to introduce spinner Paul Adams into the attack. Adams had got Freddie out at Lord's when he'd been in full flow, and Smith hoped that this might prey a little on Freddie's mind. Freddie responded by sweeping Adams's second ball for four, then hoisting him for six to take his personal score to 95 and England's total to 600 – a milestone he celebrated by high-fiving with Harmison. But, in trying to repeat the stroke next ball to take him to his 100, he was bowled. He left the middle with a smile on his face and was cheered to the echo. His 95 had come in 104 balls, with four sixes and twelve fours, and had propelled England to a lead of 120 by the time Vaughan declared shortly after Freddie was out.

Second time around, South Africa were soon in trouble, facing the swing of Bicknell and the pace of Harmison, and England had prised out six batsmen by stumps with South Africa just 65 runs ahead. Next morning the lower order succumbed fairly quickly, and in front of an ecstatic crowd cheering every run England raced to their victory target of 110 for the loss of just 1 wicket.

At the winning run it was noticeable that, at the moment of victory, the first person an elated Vaughan threw his arms around was Freddie. After his knock in a losing cause at Lord's, Freddie had said that he'd hoped he could soon play a match-winning innings for England. He hadn't quite done that at the Oval, but his 95 had certainly been a match-changing innings, not just for its value in runs but for the demoralising effect it had on the opposition at such a vital stage of the game.

In an interview after his innings, Freddie touched upon the

verbals that had been flying around during his time at the crease. 'It's been a competitive series. There have been a few words said and I don't think they think I'm very good, to be honest,' he joked. 'They question everything I do. But I've enjoyed it. They're a hard bunch of characters, at you all the time, and it's made for good fun in the middle. The one thing I've been striving for is to perform consistently with the bat, and I've done that – scored a few runs and got closer to where I want to be. I've always had it in me; it was just finding it. I feel I've matured as a batsman, worked hard and discovered what it takes to score runs at the highest level.'

The South Africans were devastated by England's fight back. They found it hard to believe that they'd lost the match after setting up such a solid platform on the first day and a half for at least the draw they needed. Never before had England conceded more than 450 in the first innings of a Test on home soil and gone on to win, and they'd accomplished it only twice overseas: once against Australia during the 1894–5 tour and once against the West Indies at Port of Spain in 1967–8.

To cap a memorable series for Freddie, he was named Man Of The Series, finishing second in the England batting averages after scoring 423 runs in his 8 innings in the five Tests, with three 50s in addition to his top score of 142 to end up with an average of 52.87. He also took ten wickets for 592 at an average of 59.20 apiece – expensive, maybe, but it was noticeable that he had bowled 20 overs more than any other

England bowler in the series and fully 40 more than spinner Ashley Giles, who also played in all five Tests. Freddie's tally of wickets would have been more and his bowling average considerably lower had England not contracted butterfingers at various times throughout the series when Freddie was bowling. Nevertheless, his overall figures showed just how far he'd come after entering the series against South Africa with a Test batting average of just 19.

The spectators who saw his exuberant Sunday exploits in the Tests at Lord's and the Oval had memories of rare hitting to treasure. Freddie had endeared himself to every England cricket follower, not least for the broad smile he allowed himself after getting out at the Oval after going for a second successive six that would have brought him his 100. Another Test century was there for the taking, but he chose to go for the big stroke and, when it didn't come off, made light of it – and the fans loved him for it.

The South African Test series took its toll on Freddie. He'd been asked to do a lot of bowling, and a groin injury forced him to miss the Tests in Bangladesh that followed just a few weeks later. He was doubly anxious to do well when he joined the One-Day squad for the Internationals, and by the end of the three-match series he had exceeded even his expectations: England had won each of the games, by the same wide margin of 7 wickets, and Freddie had been named Man Of The Match in every single one.

At Chittagong, on 7 November 2003, Freddie took a

career-best 4 wickets for 14 and belted 55, not out, from 52 balls. Three days later, at Dhaka, he thumped 70, not out, off 47 balls and equalled Ian Botham's One-Day International record of forty-four sixes. Whereas Botham had taken 116 matches to set his record, however, Freddie had taken just sixty-five.

Two days later, again at Dhaka, the scene was set for Freddie to hit his way into the record books. The crowd were full of anticipation when Freddie strode to the wicket with England needing 81 to win, and he did not disappoint, racing to a 39-ball half-century. In typically forceful style, he finished off the match with successive sixes, passing Botham's record in the process. The naming of Andrew Flintoff as Man Of The Series was a formality.

Bangladesh might have been the minnows of international cricket, but Freddie's all-round performances were consistently outstanding and put him in good heart as the team moved on to Sri Lanka and confrontations with his good friend, sometime Lancashire colleague and adversary Muralitharan.

Murali dismissed him cheaply three times before Freddie finally got to grips with the spinner in the Third and final Test. In that game, he showed he'd learned some patience, watchfully keeping Murali out and then launching into the other bowlers, hitting four sixes and ten fours, before Murali got him again for a well-struck 77.

ENGLAND v SOUTH AFRICA

Fifth npower Test, The Oval, September 4, 5, 6, 7, 8, 2003

SOUTH AFRICA	First Innings		Second Innings	
***GC Smith**	run out	**18**	lbw b Bicknell	**19**
HH Gibbs	b Giles	**183**	c Stewart b Anderson	**9**
G Kirsten	lbw b Giles	**90**	c Trescothick b Harmison	**29**
JH Kallis	run out	**66**	lbw b Harmison	**35**
ND McKenzie	c Stewart b Anderson	**9**	lbw b Flintoff	**38**
JA Rudolph	lbw b Bicknell	**0**	b Bicknell	**8**
+MB Boucher	c Stewart b Bicknell	**8**	c Stewart b Bicknell	**25**
SM Pollock	not out	**66**	c Thorpe b Harmison	**43**
AJ Hall	lbw b Flintoff	**1**	c Smith b Bicknell	**0**
	Extras	**31**		**9**
	TOTAL	**484**		**229**

FALL OF WICKETS

1/63, 2/290, 3/345, 4/362, 1/24, 2/34, 3/92, 4/93, 5/118, 5/365, 6/385, 7/419, 8/421, 6/150, 7/193, 8/193, 9/215, 9/432, 10/484, 10/229.

BOWLING

First Innings		Second Innings	
Bicknell	**20–3–71–2**	**Bicknell**	**24–5–84–4**
Anderson	**25–6–86–2**	**Anderson**	**10–1–55–1**
Harmison	**27–8–73–0**	**Harmison**	**19.2–8–33–4**
Giles	**29–3–102–2**	**Giles**	**10–2–36–0**
Flintoff	**19–4–88–1**	**Flintoff**	**6–2–13–1**
Vaughan	**5–0–24–0**		
Butcher	**3–0–18–0**		

ENGLAND	First Innings		Second Innings	
ME Trescothick	c Rudolph b Ntini	**219**	not out	**69**
***MP Vaughan**	c Gibbs b Pollock	**23**	c Boucher b Kallis	**13**
MA Butcher	lbw b Hall	**29**	not out	**20**
GP Thorpe	b Kallis	**124**		
ET Smith	lbw b Hall	**16**		
+AJ Stewart	lbw b Pollock	**38**		
A Flintoff	b Adams	**95**		
AF Giles	c Hall b Kallis	**2**		
MP Bicknell	lbw b Pollock	**0**		
SJ Harmison	not out	**6**		
JM Anderson	not out	**0**		
	Extras:	**49**		**8**
	TOTAL:	**(9 wkts dec) 604**		**(1 wkt) 110**

FALL OF WICKETS

1/47, 1/28, 2/78 3/346, 4/379, 5/480, 6/489, 7/502, 8/502, 9/601

BOWLING

First Innings		Second Innings	
Pollock	**39–10–111–3**	**Pollock**	**6–0–15–0**
Ntini	**31–4–129–1**	**Ntini**	**8–0–46–0**
Hall	**35–5–111–2**	**Kallis**	**5.2–0–25–1**
Kallis	**34–5–117–2**	**Adams**	**3–0–20–0**
Adams	**17–2–79–1**		

UMPIRES

SJA Taufel (Australia) and S Venkatraghavan (India).

Third umpire: JW Lloyds. Referee: RS Madugalle (Sri Lanka).

England won by 9 wickets. Toss: South Africa.

CHAPTER 11

A Timely Maiden

'Andrew might be a joker with the boys, but he's very romantic with me. When he proposed, earlier this year in St Lucia, he sprinkled the entire hotel room with rose petals. It was an amazing sight.'

RACHAEL WOOLS

If it's true that behind every successful man there's a good woman, it's no coincidence that Andrew Flintoff's renaissance as a supremely talented and consistent cricketer can be traced back to the arrival of Rachael Wools in his life.

Freddie met beautiful former model Rachael at an England game when she was working for Test sponsors npower in a marketing capacity. 'I fell for him because he made me laugh,' she once confided in a rare interview.

'There was an instant mutual attraction,' says a friend of them both. 'Rachael is a strikingly beautiful blonde with a fabulous figure and a dazzling smile. Freddie was knocked out by her looks, and even more so when he got to know her because she's very feminine and easy to get along with. They made a great couple from the start and everyone was really pleased when it turned out to be the real thing for them both and they decided to get married.

'Rachael's the best thing that ever happened to Freddie. Along with his commercial manager, Chubby Chandler, and his business agent, Neil Fairbrother, she brings much-needed order and purpose to his life, as well as a loving home base to come back to. With her, he's found real personal happiness, contentment and a settled domestic life. Cricket at the top can be a nomadic sort of existence, with such a crowded international calendar taking players away from home so much. Freddie needed a good woman in his life, and Rachael was and is the one.'

Freddie's love for Rachael – who had her own PR company, Strawberry Promotions – was apparent for all to see from the outset, even when he went out to bat in a Test match; for a while he'd displayed a Strawberry emblem on the back of his bat, after gaining official permission to do so. In 2003 the couple became engaged with a view to marry the following year, Freddie's busy cricket programme permitting.

Freddie decided to pop the question to Rachael when the couple were taking a working holiday in St Lucia, where Freddie was competing with Adam Hollioake in a world double-wicket competition. The Caribbean provided the perfect romantic backdrop for his wedding proposal.

In a November 2003 interview for the *News Of The World*, Rachael later talked about the transformation in her fiancé's on-field fortunes but was too modest to take the credit for clearly having had a great deal to do with it. 'Andrew was very conscious that his batting and bowling averages weren't high enough and frustrated that injuries were holding him back. People made fun of his weight, and his early reputation for good fun began to bother him, so the Andrew Flintoff you see today keeps drinking to a minimum, leaves the house early in the morning for tedious uphill runs and works his socks off with Lancashire physio Dave Roberts. He practises for hours – believe me, he's really worked at his cricket. He's changed an awful lot in a short space of time.'

As the couple scoured the calendar for possible dates for their wedding day, it became obvious that, as long as he stayed fit, almost all of 2004 would be taken up by demands on Freddie as a cricketer: a full five-Test series in the West Indies followed by a series of One-Day Internationals, then back home for Test visits from New Zealand and the West Indies, plus a full complement of One-Day Internationals, not forgetting the ICC Champions Trophy (a mini-World Cup tournament) at the climax of the English season. And that was before setting off in the autumn for a possible short tour of Zimbabwe, followed by a tour of South Africa.

First up, however, was the Caribbean, considered by many cricketers to be the toughest tour of all with searing heat, the noisiest of crowds and a gruelling itinerary of flying from island to island. Before jetting out to Jamaica, Freddie gave notice of intent by emerging top of the tree from the squad's final pre-tour fitness tests. He even promised himself that he wouldn't have a drink for the first four weeks of the tour.

Steve Harmison, however, put paid to that well-intentioned vow, courtesy of a sensational Sunday morning's play at Sabina Park in the First Test in Jamaica when he wrecked the West Indies' second innings with a superb spell of fast bowling to take 7 for 12 and bowl the hosts out for 47. England won by 10 wickets. 'There was no way I wasn't going to have a few with the lads and enjoy Steve Harmison's success,' he said with a grin. 'I had a few Red Stripes and a few rum and cokes.'

After such a glorious triumph for English cricket, and in front of a huge contingent of travelling supporters at that, celebrations were more than justified. Having so often in the past succumbed to a battery of West Indian fast bowlers in the Caribbean, England's cricketers were entitled to rejoice in the fact that the boot was now very firmly and gratifyingly on the other foot. Next morning, a distinctly hungover member of the Barmy Army assured me that he had apparently seen a jubilant Freddie throw himself, fully clothed, into the hotel swimming pool the night before by way of celebration. Mistaken identity? Probably. But, if not, a forgiveable expression of joy from a young England cricketer after a terrific win.

After the heady success of such an emphatic victory in Jamaica, the team moved on to Trinidad in fine fettle and settled in at the Hilton Hotel, perched high up on a hill in uptown Cascade, one of the smarter areas of Port of Spain. If Freddie was more jubilant than most, he was entitled to be so, after learning from an excited Rachael that she was expecting their baby. He was longing to tell everyone the good news that she was thirteen weeks pregnant but decided to keep the information quietly to himself until the Trinidad Test was over.

If Freddie or any other member of the England party needed reminding that one win doesn't constitute a series victory, and that the great Brian Lara would come hard back at them on his home Trinidad turf, they only had to look out of their hotel windows beyond the spreading branches of old samaan trees to the Queen's Park Savannah, the vast, grassy expanse that is a centrepiece of Port of Spain. There they could see, nestling imposingly in the hills above this huge city park, the magnificent house that had been custom-built for Brian Lara with Trinidad's blessing, funds and thanks for his immense contribution to Trinidad cricket. The greatness of Lara was evident even from the team hotel.

Thanks to another Man Of The Match bowling performance from Harmison, a typically battling innings from Thorpe and a first 5-wicket haul in Tests for Simon Jones, England eventually won the rain-interrupted Second Test comfortably by 7 wickets, wrapping up the win early on the fifth morning. Crucially, Lara had twice been dismissed cheaply, much to the disappointment of the locals. At this point, England had won two Test matches in a row in the

Caribbean for the first time since the 1950s, and it set them up to clinch the first series victory by an England side in the West Indies for thirty-six years.

As in the First Test, where he'd made 46 and twice took slip catches to get rid of Lara, Freddie once again made useful runs and bowled well in Trinidad. However, through no fault of his own, he found himself at the centre of an incident involving West Indies fast bowler Tino Best that rankled Freddie enough for him to carry the memory through to pay Tino back during the Lord's Test the following summer.

The incident occurred when Freddie had just come in to bat. He was facing up to his first ball when Best came running in hard, only to go through the full motions of bowling without actually holding a ball in his hand. A bemused Freddie thought he must have lost sight of a beamer, until he realised that he was the victim of a Tino prank: the ball had in fact been lodged in umpire Billy Bowdon's pocket all along.

Tino, a bouncy, effervescent, excitable character who enjoys playing the showman on the field and getting under the skin of the opposition, clearly thought that his cheeky display of gamesmanship was hilarious, and so did the West Indians in the crowd. Freddie, equally clearly, was not at all amused and told the bowler so, in no uncertain terms. It made for a fiery confrontation in the ensuing overs, but Freddie weathered the storm and kept his head – and had the last laugh over Tino four months later at Lord's.

The early finish to the Trinidad Test on the fifth morning

at the Queen's Park Oval allowed England's victorious players to take up the offer of Hampshire chairman, Rod Bransgrove, to celebrate by spending the afternoon on his magnificent yacht off the west coast of Trinidad before the party moved on to Barbados. It was a high-spirited group of cricketers who enjoyed the hospitality, swam and took turns to skim through the waves on jetskis. Two–nil up in the series, the players were already cock-a-hoop when Freddie took the celebrations up a notch aboard the yacht by revealing to his teammates that he was to become a father.

Later, as the jet carrying them all triumphantly out of Trinidad roared down the runway at Piarco Airport and nosed into the sky, the mood of the party was heartened still further by the knowledge that wives and loved ones would soon be flying into Barbados to join them on the next leg of the tour. For Freddie, it was going to be a particularly poignant reunion with Rachael, now that she was carrying his child. Also, although he didn't know it yet, his brother Chris was planning to fly in unannounced from Japan to watch the Third Test. On their arrival, the personal support of Rachael and Chris made Freddie all the more determined to put in a special performance.

Thus far in the series, it had been Harmison who'd captured all the headlines and the lion's share of West Indian wickets. But, as Brian Lara had confided to Nasser Hussain, the pace and bounce that Freddie had been extracting offered no relief to himself and his fellow West Indian batsmen once they'd seen off Harmison, Hoggard and Jones. Freddie was proving a handful, no doubt about it – and at Barbados he finally had the figures to prove it.

It had become something of a joke among the England party that Freddie invariably bowled the most overs and yet, in his thirty-two Tests, he had still to record a 5-wicket haul. It was something that the press liked to point out and that Freddie himself was all too aware of. It was a situation he was anxious to put right.

At the Kensington Oval, the West Indies batted first and Freddie seized his chance, pitching the ball well up and bowling accurately, intelligently and fast. First he had Lara pushing uncertainly forward, to be caught by Butcher in the slips. Next he had Shivnarine Chanderpaul taken by Thorpe at slip feeling for a wide one, then produced a ball for the gutsy wicketkeeper-batsman Ridley Jacobs that reared up at his throat and which he could only fend off for a simple catch. Another short ball pinned Tino Best on the back foot and induced a catch gloved from in front of his face.

Freddie now had 4 wickets, and the sight of Fidel Edwards walking to the wicket and taking guard must have filled him with the hope that he could roll him over quickly. Edwards might be a bowler of raw pace, but he was no Lara with the bat.

Each one of Freddie's 4 wickets had been cheered to the echo by the 12,000 England supporters who had swarmed into the ground. West Indian supporters were hopelessly outnumbered and the stands around the ground were covered in flags of St George. The more clued-up of the English support knew that Freddie had never taken 5 wickets in a Test, and the ground was buzzing with expectation as he prepared to bowl at Edwards. He was roared each step of the way on his run-up to the wicket and the ground erupted in thunderous applause when Freddie dismissed Edwards first ball, snicking a catch through to Chris Read behind the stumps. Freddie punched the air in joy as teammates rushed from their fielding positions to congratulate him.

The West Indies had been dismissed for a lowly 224 on the first day thanks to Freddie's 5 for 58, only the second 5-for he'd ever taken in his First-Class career. Invited to lead the team off the field after his efforts with the ball, Freddie's smile was matched by that of the coach. The normally taciturn Duncan Fletcher was positively beaming, almost laughing.

Graham Thorpe kept England in the match with a brilliant century, and then, in the West Indies' second innings, it was Matthew Hoggard's turn for a slice of the bowling glory. He took a hat-trick, and had the good sense to achieve it by inducing the third of his victims to edge a catch into the very safe hands of Andrew Flintoff in the slips. Freddie would never have forgiven himself if he'd spilled it.

Poor Lara could only watch the devastation from the non-striker's end. When Hoggard completed his hat-trick, the West Indies captain sat down on his backside with his head between his knees. His side were shot out for 94 and England completed their third victory out of three to win the series. It had been a fabulous team effort, and on the lap of honour to thank the England fans for their phenomenal support there were cries from the stands of 'Freddie's got a 5-for!'

Three–nil down and demoralised, Lara's West Indian team were desperate to salvage some pride and deprive the visitors of a whitewash by preventing England from winning the final Test in Antigua. This was the ground where Lara had set his Test-record score of 375, and one look at the Antigua wicket was enough to convince the more seasoned cricket correspondents to declare that the strip looked almost the same, and just as flat and as full of runs, as it had when Lara had previously amassed his record total. And so it proved.

England's bowlers, Harmison included, were blunted by the pitch and Lara's determination to bat England out of the game. In an innings of monumental concentration, the left-handed genius batted his way flawlessly (apart from a half-chance to Gareth Batty) to an incredible 400, not out. Only Brian Charles Lara could produce a second record score on the same ground as his first, and against the same opposition.

On such a flat wicket, the West Indies were unlikely to bowl England out twice, but nevertheless the game still had to be saved and Freddie showed great restraint and responsibility in riding his luck to compile a patient 102, not out, in five-and-a-half hours to pilot England to safety. He later said that when he'd reached his 100 he'd felt almost too embarrassed to raise his bat in acknowledgement of the milestone after Lara had scored four times as many.

That innings wasn't one of Freddie's best, but it was important to the team, and the England fans – once again arrayed in vast numbers around the ground – rose to him. Among them, there was none prouder than Colin and Susan Flintoff, who had flown in to join Rachael in Antigua.

Freddie had shown real consistency in all facets of his game throughout the series in the Caribbean, and it was just the start of what was to become a golden 2004.

CHAPTER 12

A Golden Summer

'I saw the ball all the way and should have caught it. But I'm glad he wasn't the first Test batsman to be caught by his dad. He wouldn't have been able to stop laughing, and that would have been the end of him!'

COLIN FLINTOFF AFTER A MASSIVE SIX BY FREDDIE DROPPED INTO HIS HANDS AND OUT AGAIN IN THE RYDER STAND AT EDGBASTON DURING ENGLAND'S SECOND TEST AGAINST THE WEST INDIES, 2004

No one would ever question what Nasser Hussain did for English cricket. He played with unswerving passion, with his heart on his sleeve, he always gave his all in the middle and, as captain of the national side, he transformed England from being an undisciplined, unprofessional outfit into a team with some much-needed backbone and fight.

Freddie has never been backward in praising Nasser as a great captain for England. Indeed, the all-rounder might have drifted out of Test cricket as a failure if Nasser hadn't kept faith in him at a time when Freddie was his own worst enemy. 'I fell out of favour with some of the England people, but Nasser always stuck by me through thick and thin,' he has admitted, 'and I'll never forget that as long as I live. Nasser Hussain has proved a major influence on my career. Even when I had my bad days – especially in India, when I couldn't even spell "bat" – he always had faith in my ability when maybe some wouldn't.'

As it turned out, the purple patch that Freddie came to enjoy on the major cricket fields of England in 2004 coincided with Michael Vaughan taking over the captaincy and introducing a new style of leadership whereby the team were encouraged to play with a smile and without a fear of failure.

Given more freedom to express himself, Freddie flourished spectacularly in a 2004 English summer that saw England beat a well-led, experienced New Zealand side three–nil and follow up with a four–nil series victory over the West Indies. Freddie was in the form of his life, and he lit up the summer almost every time he went out to bat. When he briefly had to withdraw from England's One-Day side with a persistent ankle problem, they struggled without him. 'We can win games with Andrew Flintoff and we will win games without Andrew Flintoff,' Vaughan said bravely after Freddie had injured his ankle, but the truth is that England didn't win games in the NatWest One-Day series without Freddie. And, when he returned to the team as a batsman only, he was magnificent.

Freddie's form and his prodigious hitting had fans flocking through the turnstiles to see him in action. He was the biggest cricket draw in a summer of unprecedented Test success for England, and the crowds loved him and the entertaining way he made his runs.

In the Lord's Test against the West Indies, a rare failure produced surely the loudest collective sigh of disappointment from a full house ever to have echoed around the old ground. After Robert Key had plundered a double century on a flat wicket, Freddie announced himself by driving the young off-spinner Omri Banks straight back over his head for six, setting the crowd buzzing and eagerly anticipating more. But then he got out the very next ball, over-reaching outside off-stump for another drive without quite getting to the pitch of the ball and edging it into his stumps. The 20,000 gasps of dismay uttered in unison by a packed Lord's could probably have been heard as far away as Oxford Street.

Making his way back through the pavilion to the dressing room, Freddie received a smart rap on the back by an MCC member using a rolled-up newspaper and the rebuke, 'That was good while it lasted.' Such was Freddie's rich vein of form that even MCC members felt robbed when their hero got himself out cheaply. However, a smooth half-century in the second innings had the members purring once again and helped to pave the way for victory, along with a priceless moment for Freddie that had its origins in Trinidad, back in March, when Freddie had been duped by Tino Best's fake-bowling antics.

This time it was Tino's turn to look foolish. In the first innings, Freddie had had the pleasure of sending Best's off stump cartwheeling out of the ground with a fast delivery. Now, second time around, Best was making his way out to the middle to face up to spinner Ashley Giles. Before the little fast bowler prepared to take guard, from his position at slip Freddie joked, 'Watch those windows, Tino,' inviting him to have a slog towards the windows of the Media Centre at the Nursery End. Best immediately charged down the wicket to take a swing at Giles, was hopelessly beaten in the flight and was stumped by a country mile. Freddie simply couldn't contain himself and roared with laughter.

Lara's men came to Edgbaston for the Second Test with new focus, but ran up against Freddie in vintage form as he produced one of the innings of the season. The game was nicely poised on the first day when the West Indies reduced England to 262 for 5 and Freddie came to the crease determined to be there still with his wicket intact at the close of play. He had moved into the 40s by stumps and got his head down for the team to such good effect that, in the car park after play, a spectator spotted him and knocked on his car window to enquire of Freddie whether the wicket was proving tricky to bat on, as he had appeared so subdued and hadn't produced his customary fireworks.

Next day, Freddie's parents were among a capacity crowd of 20,000 and settled down in the front row of the upper deck of the Ryder Stand, hoping to watch their son build on his good start of the previous evening and play a big innings. The omens looked good when Freddie cover-drove his first ball to the boundary. Luck also appeared to be with him when a couple of flashes flew over Lara at slip, and when he was on

71 Freddie offered a return catch to Jermaine Lawson, who put it down. It was to prove a costly miss.

When he passed 50, Freddie became the first England player since Alec Stewart in 1996 to do so in six successive Tests, and soon he was giving full rein to his range of powerful strokes. With Geraint Jones playing fluently at the other end, the pair took the game away from the West Indies. Lara and his bowlers were unable to stem the flow of runs, and Freddie provided one of the enduring images of the summer when he hoisted Lawson for six over long on.

As Freddie completed the shot, his eyes followed the ball's trajectory, high over the long-on boundary, and saw a spectator in a white shirt rise up from his seat as the ball fell towards him. He knew his dad was up in the Ryder Stand where the ball was falling and suddenly realised who was waiting directly underneath his big hit. To Freddie's amusement, he watched Colin get his hands to the ball but fumble it, deflecting it into the lap of Michael Vaughan's mum, Dee, sitting in the row behind.

The parabola of the 'dropped catch' and its remarkable Flintoff family connection was followed all the way by the television cameras, and its outcome made for much jokey comment at the end of play. 'My dad plays at weekends, and he's always coming home and telling me about the great catches he's held,' chuckled Freddie. 'Well, today he proved to everyone that he's really terrible at catching!'

Colin also saw the funny side, even though he'd spilled the

catch in front of millions of viewers. 'I saw the ball all the way and should have caught it. But I'm glad he wasn't the first Test batsman to be caught by his dad. He wouldn't have been able to stop laughing, and that would have been the end of him!'

With Geraint Jones, Freddie put on 170 and added a further 46 with Giles. And when Giles got out, Freddie felt it was time to press his foot on the pedal and really go after the bowling, with the inexperienced off-spin of Banks his prime target. Poor Banks watched three balls in one over disappear into the far distance for a trio of sixes – all from perfectly executed shots. Freddie powered on to make 167, his highest Test score, eclipsing his 142 against South Africa. It was also his highest score in First-Class cricket, beating his 160 against Yorkshire in 1999.

In all, Freddie batted for 191 balls over four-and-a-half hours and hit seventeen fours and seven sixes before finally falling LBW to the persevering Dwayne Bravo's slower ball, having set up a winning platform.

Bravo, a young all-rounder with great potential, later explained to me how difficult it had been to bowl to Freddie that day. 'In our team meetings we talked about the strengths and weaknesses of all the players in the England team, and we knew with Andrew that, once he gets going, he's so hard to bowl to. We know he doesn't like to hang around, and what we tried to do was play a waiting game and let him come at us. But that day he changed the game; he hit the ball with such power, and I was so pleased to get him out.

'Freddie's a great player, a tremendous player, someone I look up to, and we became good friends during the series. I went to him for advice and he gave it to me and shared his experience with me.'

England were able to declare at Edgbaston on 566 for 9 and went on to crush the West Indies by 256 runs, with Hoggard and Giles sharing the majority of the wickets.

Freddie's memorable knock prompted some cricket pundits to wonder whether he was now the best cricketer in the world, when his bowling and brilliant slip-fielding were taken into consideration alongside his destructive batting, and in the run-up to the Third Test at Old Trafford, Michael Vaughan was inclined to agree. 'At the minute, he's on the crest of a wave, playing exceptionally well. People talk about him being a powerful hitter, but not a lot of people mention what a good technique he has. The crowd here will obviously go mad when he goes out to the wicket, but he's got to try to control his emotions. If he can do that, the way he's playing he'll get another big score.'

Vaughan agreed that self-discipline had been the key to Freddie's remarkable transformation. 'That's the progression of Freddie over the last year. A year or so ago, he'd be the first to admit that, when the crowd roared, he'd try and hit the first ball out of the ground for six, get 20-odd and then get out. He's learned a hell of a lot from that and his experiences. Someone mentioned the other day that he's the best cricketer in the world at the minute, and I'm not going to argue with that.'

Freddie had every incentive to carry his wonderful form into the Third Test at Old Trafford. He had previously played just one Test on his home ground, against Sri Lanka in 2002, when he'd been unluckily run out for a single. Now he was looking forward to playing there again in front of family and friends, especially as he'd made just the one appearance at Old Trafford all season, in a limited-overs game for Lancashire.

England arrived at Old Trafford two–nil up, and another victory would clinch the series. They duly achieved it with yet another half-century from Freddie when England chased down 231 in the second innings in overcast conditions. England had trailed by 65 runs in the first innings, but they bowled out the West Indies for 165 second time around. Freddie was in good form with the ball, cleverly bowling Lara behind his legs after observing that the great man had a habit of moving too far across his crease and leaving his leg stump exposed. Freddie figured that he could bowl him out with a fast leg-stump yorker, and the plan worked to perfection.

England were 111 for 3 in pursuit of the 231 victory target when Freddie joined his old England Under-Nineteens pal Robert Key, who was playing well and showing composure. As the target was whittled down, it eventually became clear that a century was there for Key's taking if Freddie gave his partner as much of the strike as possible, and eventually 10 were needed for victory, with Key on 90. Freddie generously offered to block the bowling to allow Key to reach three figures, but the Kent man was having none of it and told him to finish the match as soon as possible. A full toss from Sarwan that Freddie smacked back over the bowler's head settled that issue, and the two of them saw England safely home with Key 93, not out. For Freddie, being there at the crease at the end to help England win the series on his home ground was one of the highlights of the season.

As in the Caribbean earlier in the year, the West Indies were desperate to avoid a whitewash in the Test series when the teams moved on to the Oval for the Fourth Test, but this time there was no escape and a rampant England won comfortably to complete seven Test wins out of seven that summer.

Freddie was named Man Of The Series for his 387 runs and 14 wickets, but he conceded that either Steve Harmison or Ashley Giles were just as deserving. Team man to the last, after England had bowled the West Indies out at the Oval for the last time, Freddie made a point of going up to every single one of his teammates and giving them each a hug in turn. And, in the most generous and thoughtful of gestures, he later ran over to give his Man Of The Series champagne to a woman in the crowd with multiple sclerosis who he and the other England players had got talking to before the start of play. When he spotted her and her husband again at the end of the day, he decided she should have the bubbly, later saying that the couple would put it to much better use than pouring it over Steve Harmison's head.

If Freddie showed impressive consistency laced with moments of sheer brilliance in the summer's two Test series, his form in the various limited-overs internationals was nothing short of sensational. He hit a dazzling 106 off 121 balls against New Zealand at Bristol and followed up by belting 123 in 104 balls at Lord's against the West Indies in one of the most brutal and entertaining displays of power-hitting a Lord's crowd are ever likely to see. His incredible innings included no less than seven huge sixes.

Then, against India in the first of three One-Day Internationals, he smashed 34, not out, off 23 balls at Trent Bridge, including a towering six off Kumble to win the match. It was an important innings in the context of Freddie's past struggles against the Indian spinners and, while it had been only a cameo, he'd thrown down a marker and shown them he was a very different player from the lead-footed, tentative Flintoff they'd encountered in 2001–2.

Any remaining doubts of Freddie's pre-eminence in the game were swept away in the second match against India at the Oval, where Freddie fell for 99 after another terrific innings. Having whacked Sehwag for six, he could have taken a single to bring up his 100 but instead went for another huge hit and succeeded only in top-edging a steepling catch to the wicketkeeper. At a time when it seemed he could do no wrong on the cricket field, it was no surprise that it was Freddie who took the final wicket to ensure that England won the series.

England could have done with him in the third and final NatWest Challenge match against India, but that day Freddie had a far more pressing engagement: the birth of his first child. He had been attending ante-natal classes with his fiancée, Rachael, and absolutely nothing was going to stop him from being at her side during the actual birth.

Freddie was there to cut the cord when Rachael duly gave birth to Holly, who arrived weighing in at 6lb 2oz at 4am on Monday, 6 September 2004, and, after Freddie had rung round his and Rachael's family, his great pal Steve Harmison was among the first people he telephoned to pass on the good news. 'He rang me at 4:53 am,' said Steve. 'I'm really happy for him – though I wasn't at the time. My phone was lighting up and I thought it was my alarm. I answered it and he just said, "I'm a dad!" I know what he's going through, and it's a special time. He'll be on one hell of a high at Edgbaston.'

England lost to India at Lord's while Freddie was away on paternity leave, but he rejoined the squad for the opening ICC Champions Trophy game against Zimbabwe four days later, when he took 3 for 11 in 6 overs to show the team what they'd been missing.

Next, his batting was once again the match-winning factor in what was to all intents and purposes an ICC Champions Trophy quarter-final clash with Sri Lanka at Southampton's Rose Bowl. Dropped before he'd even scored, Freddie's touch seemed to have completely deserted him, but rain meant that the game went into a second day and Freddie re-emerged the following day at full, glorious throttle to hit a century in 91 balls, his second 50 coming in only 20 balls. On that occasion, he hit nine fours and three sixes and went to three figures with a delicate late cut. It was his third 100 in six One-Day Internationals and, after more rain, England went through on the Duckworth-Lewis method.

The most welcome of victories over Australia took England into the final against the West Indies at the Oval, which Lara's men won in thrilling fashion after seemingly heading for defeat. A turning point in the match was Lara pulling off a stunning catch at mid-on to dismiss Freddie for just 3. Later Freddie had his revenge over Lara with the ball, but it wasn't enough and, in fading autumnal light, the West Indies squeezed home.

It was a disappointing end to the season for the England squad, but followers of English cricket could nevertheless reflect on a summer of record success at Test level – and a golden summer for their champion all-rounder. Freddie had scored a half-century in each of the home Tests, and the lasting images of the season were of him freeing his arms to strike the ball with awesome power to huge distances with beautifully executed cricket shots.

In a rare game away from the international arena, Freddie smashed 85 off 48 balls during a televised Twenty20 Cup match between Lancashire and Yorkshire. In the middle of this mayhem, viewers heard umpire Ian Gould quip, 'The safety officer has just rung to say, "Can Flintoff get out? Everyone's in danger here, mate!"'

To round off a memorable few months, two days after his daughter was born, Freddie was named International One-

Day Cricketer of the Year at the ICC's inaugural cricket 'Oscars' ceremony at London's Alexandra Palace. He was also deservedly named in the World One-Day XI of the Year, and soon afterwards his fellow professionals voted him Players' Player of the Year.

CHAPTER 13

The History Man

'I'm not blind to what's happening in the world, and the situation in Zimbabwe looks bad.'

ANDREW FLINTOFF, EXPLAINING IN THE SUN WHY HE WOULDN'T BE GOING ON ENGLAND'S 2004 TOUR TO ZIMBABWE

Throughout England's triumphant summer of 2004, one dilemma lurked largely unresolved in the back of the minds of all the players in the squad. England were scheduled to make a short tour of Zimbabwe before moving on to the much bigger task of taking on South Africa on their own soil. The question the players were asking themselves was an extremely personal one: if selected, would they be prepared to tour Zimbabwe?

There wasn't much open discussion on the subject, but all summer there were rumours that three, possibly four, star England names would choose not to go to Zimbabwe. The word was that Steve Harmison would definitely not be touring and that Freddie would also abstain, along with maybe Ashley Giles.

Putting the political aspect of the tour completely to one side, it seemed sensible, if not imperative, that the opportunity should be taken to give several of England's leading players a well-earned rest. This applied especially to Freddie, after his ankle problems, and to Harmison, who by the end of the English season was officially rated as the world's number-one bowler. Shorn of their leading players, caught up in the continuing political situation in their country and the disputes about team selection, the Zimbabwe team was most unlikely to pose much of a challenge in the Test arena. It therefore made sense to give key England players a break in a series that was expected to be a mismatch. In the event, Zimbabwe's shortage of enough players of quality to compete at Test level led to the Tests being scrapped and the tour reduced to just One-Day Internationals.

The situation offered an obvious chance for Harmison to put his feet up for a while after a hard year. A couple of months away from the game would give him time to recharge his batteries so that he was fresh and raring to go to take on the Springboks.

The same could be said of Freddie, who had bowled as many, if not more, overs for his country in Tests than any other England bowler during the year and had been troubled by ankle problems in the summer. Flushed by England's success in the Test matches, England's fans – and even some pundits – were already looking ahead one year to the battle for the Ashes and crying excitedly, 'Bring on the Aussies!' Wiser heads, notably that of Shane Warne, were counselling caution. Let's just see how England shape up in twelve months, said the legendary Australian spinner. Let's see if England's key players all remain fit when the Tests start in July 2005.

The warning could hardly have been plainer. Warne pointed out that, with such a congested and relentless international calendar, England treasures such as Harmison and Flintoff needed careful handling if they were to reach the Ashes Tests in top condition, ready to take on the best team in the world. 'England have to make sure now that they don't destroy Flintoff,' Warne cautioned in an end-of-season review in *The Times*. 'Because he is hard to score off, with his height and angle, there might be a temptation to use him as a stock bowler. That could be wrong and have terrible consequences.' They were prophetic words indeed.

While Harmison would have been rested for Zimbabwe, the Durham paceman declared that he wouldn't be going anyway, thus pre-empting the selectors' decision before the touring party was finalised. Also missing when the tour party was announced was the name of Andrew Flintoff, who the selectors, coach and management explained had earned a rest. Wisely, they had planned all along to give Freddie a break, but Freddie waited until the end of the season to inform coach Duncan Fletcher and captain Michael Vaughan of his decision: that he would abstain from the tour on moral grounds.

Freddie could have hidden behind the selectors' decision to give him an extended break, but commendably he wanted to make it known that he'd chosen not to go because of a moral responsibility. And it wasn't long before he went on to explain in an interview in the *Sun* precisely how and why he'd arrived at his decision.

Like Harmison, Freddie said that he'd made up his mind eighteen months earlier, when the players had endured those three extraordinary days in Cape Town, debating the rights and wrongs of playing their opening 2003 World Cup game in Zimbabwe, a country whose cruel regime saw its people starved, murdered and forcibly driven from their homes.

Freddie and the rest of the England squad had taken up cricket in their youth as a game to be enjoyed. Back then, they'd never thought that one day, as elite international players, they'd find themselves sitting in Cape Town, engulfed in an international political crisis and pulled in different directions by government ministers and cricket's top officials, spending three days doing little more than discussing matters of life and death in protracted, fraught meetings. The ordeal reduced some players to tears.

The British government didn't want the players to go to Zimbabwe but wouldn't go so far as to order them not to play there – which threw the ball back into the court of cricket's officials and presented all the players with a dilemma of conscience.

To make matters worse, the team had been sent a very serious death threat that they would go home in wooden coffins or have to live in fear for the rest of their lives if they went to Zimbabwe. There was also the very real fear of bloodshed if demonstrators came to the ground and were beaten or arrested for their protests.

As England captain Nasser Hussain succinctly outlined in his autobiography, *Playing With Fire*, Freddie and Ashley Giles, while both recuperating from injuries in England, had both viewed a documentary on Channel 4 that highlighted shocking aspects of Robert Mugabe's regime in Zimbabwe. When the two players flew out to join the other members of the World Cup squad, the two players relayed what they'd seen and indicated they wouldn't be going to Zimbabwe even if the ICC tried to force them.

It was a decision that Freddie and Giles hadn't arrived at lightly. To play in the World Cup is one of the great challenges for any top cricketer, and the England players knew they would almost certainly be throwing away the chance of winning the trophy if they failed to play the Zimbabwe game.

Eighteen months later, Freddie pointed out in an interview with the *Sun*'s John Etheridge that he felt nothing had changed since the meetings and problems the squad had faced in Cape Town before the World Cup. 'In fact,' he said, 'from everything I've read and heard, things have got worse in Zimbabwe. Most of us have seen images from the African country and the situation looks horrific. I'm not blind to what's happening in the world, and the situation in Zimbabwe looks bad.'

Freddie recalled that, in those endless meetings in Cape

Town, the players had had to consider what might happen to anyone who chose to turn up at England's games to make peaceful demonstrations. The risk was that they would be treated badly, and Freddie didn't want that on his conscience.

In going public on his reasons for not touring, Freddie wanted it to be known exactly how he felt, although he made it clear that he had nothing against the players who had decided to go to Zimbabwe. For their part, the England and Wales Cricket Board promised players that they wouldn't be discriminated against if they withdrew from the tour.

For the England players, one glance at the itinerary showed just how physically demanding the forthcoming tour of South Africa would be. Partly because South Africa had just played Zimbabwe after coming back from touring India, the five Tests would be crammed into the tightest of series schedules, including back-to-back Tests at the start and end. Then, once the Test series was over, the players would soon afterwards embark on a series of seven One-Day Internationals in fourteen days at seven different venues.

Squeezed into just under six weeks, the Tests would inevitably be a series of unrelenting intensity. And the only real respite afforded to the players to recover from injuries, or simply to rest aching limbs, would be the seven days off between the Third and Fourth Tests.

On this tour, unlike previous tours, there would be no provincial fixtures between the Tests. This meant that any batsman out of touch or any bowler striving for rhythm would have no opportunity between the Tests to play themselves back into form out in the middle. Their only chance to find form would come in the nets.

In addition, those players, like Freddie, who hadn't taken part in the tour of Zimbabwe would be expected to hit the ground running with no time for acclimatisation. They'd get just one week's preparation in neighbouring Namibia, owing to South Africa refusing to provide any opposition for practice matches. This would be followed by a solitary warm-up game against South Africa A before the Test series started.

The players were aware they'd have to find their form swiftly – and strive to keep it. Once the Test series got under way, every single match thereafter would be an international, either a Test or a One-Day game. In effect, every game was to be a big one, and England's players were being asked to perform at the highest level with only minimal preparation.

To get himself fit for such an arduous tour, come early November Freddie was conscientiously preparing his body for the rigours ahead. In addition to going through his normal fitness routines, most mornings he was to be found slugging punchbags, pounding the pads, shadow-boxing and sparring at Oliver's Gym, home of Salford Boxing Club, near Manchester. He had been introduced to the gym a year earlier by Lancashire colleague Iain Sutcliffe, a boxing blue at Oxford.

Former England wicketkeeper Warren Hegg, another Lancashire colleague, was an acquaintance of boxing promoter Steve Wood and put Freddie in touch with the gym, where the pugilists gave the cricketer a warm welcome. He took his place there energetically, training alongside such fighters as WBU middleweight champion Anthony Farnell and featherweight Steve Foster, while a poster of Mike Tyson – a sports idol of Freddie's in his youth – stared menacingly down from the wall.

This was no light, token workout; Freddie took the training extremely seriously, putting himself through one particularly gruelling exercise under the watchful eye of veteran trainer Jed Livesey that involved Freddie leaping forty times a minute from one side to the other over a metal bar positioned almost at waist height. His target on his trips to the gym were an energy-sapping 200 such jumps. He also spent time skipping, which not only worked up a sweat but also would be beneficial, he reckoned, in keeping him light on his feet and aid his foot movement when batting, while the sparring helped with his foot, hand and eye co-ordination.

When he wasn't putting himself through punishing training sessions, he was able to spend some much-cherished time with baby Holly, whose name – along with that of Rachael – he had proudly tattooed on the top of his left arm. He also emerged from the tattooist with an upper right arm decorated with the Roman numerals 'XI', his England-squad number.

When it came to assessing the opposition, England were under no illusions about the task that lay ahead in South Africa. Following their recent successes, they would arrive officially ranked as the second-best international Test team in the world, behind Australia, and at a time when South Africa – rated at number six in the ICC Test Championship rankings – were in a rebuilding process.

England were favourites to win, but they would be up against a team who were always difficult to beat in their own back yard. History showed that England hadn't won a series in South Africa since the 1964–5 tour captained by Mike Smith, fully forty years earlier. And, since South Africa's return from their Test-match isolation of the apartheid era, they'd lost at home only to Australia.

Traditionally, England v South Africa has always been a tough contest. The Springboks always played hard and would be formidable opponents, skippered by Graeme Smith, a young captain who had led from the front in England eighteen months earlier. 'We've got a fighting spirit, a tradition of never making it easy for others,' warned South Africa's abrasive new coach Ray Jennings. 'We won't lie down.'

It was a warning heeded. Prior to the South Africa tour, Freddie cautioned that England could undo all their good work of 2004 if the team failed to come up to scratch against the South Africans, telling *Sport On Five*, 'I think we deserve to be number two in the world. We've played good cricket in the last eighteen months to get there. It's been a real team effort, and everyone at some point has played a part in an England victory. But, if we don't play well in South Africa, that will soon be forgotten.'

Looking back over the previous twelve months, he said, 'It's been a great year, the birth of the baby being the highlight. I've managed to be part of a successful side with England, and I've managed to contribute to what's been happening. I've got a settled home life. I'm happy at home and I'm happy with my cricket. I've learned a better way of going about things. I think that's evidenced on the pitch.

'I've got a technique in which I trust and a method and approach for preparing an innings which is 100 times better than it used to be. The bowling is getting slightly better. I'm still a novice in some ways, but I feel I'm improving, and Troy Cooley, the bowling coach, has helped in that respect.'

As a batsman, Freddie was looking forward to renewing his battles with fast bowlers Makhaya Ntini and Shaun Pollock. And, as a bowler, he would be pitting himself against a formidable line-up headed by Herschelle Gibbs, Graeme Smith and the great Jacques Kallis, who for many would be an automatic choice in a World XI.

Inevitably, during the build-up to the series, copious comparisons were being made between the great all-rounders on either side: Freddie for England and Kallis for South Africa. With an overall batting average of 54 and on the crest of a wave after a magnificent year with the bat, averaging at around 80, Kallis was undoubtedly one of the globe's best batsmen and was officially rated second in world Test-batting rankings. But the word coming back to the England camp was that, although he'd been an essential part of South Africa's attack over the past few years and had taken crucial wickets, he was now something of a less threatening performer with the ball.

One thing, however, was certain: South African cricket fans were looking forward to watching Freddie bat. His reputation for big-hitting preceded him; the South Africans remembered his innings of 142 at Lord's and his game-changing 95 at the Oval on South Africa's last tour of England, and the connoisseurs were aware of just how destructive his batting could be. Barry Richards, the brilliant former South Africa opening bat, openly warned home supporters, 'Two hours of Flintoff and he can take the game away from anybody.'

England's tour didn't get off to the best of starts, with the team losing rather too easily to South Africa A, and the general opinion was that England were coming into the First Test match at St George's Park, Port Elizabeth, distinctly undercooked. During that game, South Africa posted a decent first-innings score of 337, with Freddie returning good figures of 3 top-order wickets for 72. England then replied with 425, thanks largely to 126 from opener Andrew Strauss. Freddie contributed a useful 35 but looked to be below his best – and it was apparent, while he was at the crease, that he felt that way, too. After safely negotiating a tricky period in the middle, he allowed himself to emit an audible 'Yes!' in sheer relief when he finally threw off the shackles by driving a ball through the covers to the boundary.

In South Africa's second innings, Freddie took 2 for 47 to help dismiss the opposition for 229, thus leaving England needing 141 to win. Freddie started South Africa's slide when he induced captain Graeme Smith into pulling a ball to deep fine leg, where Simon Jones took a wonderful running catch down by his bootlaces. Thanks to another polished and assured innings of 94, not out, by Strauss, England waltzed to victory by 7 wickets.

After the match, there was much jubilation in the England dressing room, where the feeling was that they'd managed to pull off an ultimately emphatic win while performing at what they felt was no more than seventy per cent of their best. And with England coming into the First Test so short of proper match practice, it seemed that South Africa had lost their best chance in the series of putting one over the opposition. Not only was it a great start for England, the victory was their eighth in succession – a record for an England Test team.

An ever-present member of the team, Freddie could take satisfaction from the fact that he'd played an important part in a victorious sequence that had begun in March, when Steve Harmison had destroyed the West Indies in Jamaica. Now the record had been broken on South African soil and the players had given each other the perfect Christmas present. With fiancée Rachael and her parents bringing baby Holly with them to join up with Freddie for Holly's first Christmas after a trip to Sun City, everything was rosy in the Flintoff camp. The sight of the giant figure of Freddie – a popular figure anyway – pushing his little daughter around in her pushchair made for a touching scene.

In chilly England on 26 December 2004, Freddie's glorious straight drives and effortless pulls for six were once again lighting up television screens across the country, but unfortunately this was a Channel 4 Boxing Day flashback to Freddie's summer fireworks in England, not Freddie out in the middle in Durban. On the very day that TV viewers in England were being treated to a retrospective glimpse of Flintoff's magnificent clean hitting, the big man himself wasn't exactly distinguishing himself on the first day of the Second Test match.

Remarkably, Freddie's explosive hitting had been voted into forty-fourth place in Channel 4's list of *100 Greatest TV Treats Of 2004* – a measure of his huge popularity with the British public – but at the sun-baked Kingsmead Cricket Ground in Durban, it was a very different story. There, Freddie was trudging back to the pavilion for a duck.

England were put in to bat by Graeme Smith and were then bundled out for 139 in just 57.1 overs. It was an unexpected start to an enthralling match that would see-saw one way and then the other, almost bringing an away win to rival England's Botham-inspired comeback at Headingley in 1981.

England's poor first-innings total at Kingsmead was perhaps due in part to a little complacency, but also certainly to some fine bowling by Pollock and Ntini, aided by some injudicious shots by England's batsmen on a pitch that appeared to be a corrugated strip, making batting difficult. It was England's lowest first-innings total for fifty-nine Tests and gave South Africa a golden chance to follow up their bowling performance to build a big score and level the series.

Flintoff got out without troubling the scorers when he mistimed a hook off Shaun Pollock, who cramped him up as he went through with his shot, the ball ballooning up off the splice of his bat to present an easy catch to debutant Hashim Amla. By the end of a day that belonged almost entirely to South Africa after England's batting collapse, there was some consolation for Freddie when he comfortably pouched a catch at slip to dismiss Graeme Smith cheaply, thereby helping Steve Harmison to equal Ian Botham's outstanding record of taking 63 Test-match wickets in a calendar year.

Thanks to a magnificent 162 from Kallis, his eighteenth Test century, South Africa built a seemingly impregnable lead of 193. In just over six hours at the crease, Kallis was beaten just the once – by Freddie, who went on to return the respectable figures in such a big total of 2 wickets for 66 runs in 23 overs, all bowled under an unforgiving sun that was frying the sky. The temperature was up to thirty-three degrees and, coupled with so much humidity, at least another ten degrees could be added to what the players were feeling. Moreover, an additional onus was on Freddie and the other seamers to perform well and draw on the depths of their stamina because Ashley Giles had had to leave the field, unable to bowl after suffering spasms in his back.

England had their backs to the wall as Kallis ground down the bowling, but Freddie at least had the pleasing sight of Martin van Jaarsveld's middle stump flying out of the ground from one of his fuller deliveries.

With such a huge deficit of runs to make up, England faced a mammoth task. It would need one, two, possibly three batsmen to make big 100s and post a total of 400 or more if they were to have any hope of saving the game. In the event, three of the top five made 100s, with Marcus Trescothick and Andrew Strauss posting a terrific opening stand of 273, full of fine strokeplay, before being parted.

Despite this wonderful opening partnership, England weren't completely out of the woods, and when Freddie came to the crease at 314 for 4 on the fourth morning of the match they were wobbling slightly, the game in the balance once more after Michael Vaughan and Mark Butcher had both been lost cheaply.

At that stage, England were only 121 runs ahead with something like 160 overs left to be bowled in the match. Another couple of quick wickets and South Africa would have been very much back in the match and with a chance of winning. It was therefore vital for England that Flintoff played a responsible innings and built a partnership with a rusty Grahame Thorpe. The Surrey left-hander was playing only his fifth innings since August but was now beginning to show signs of finding his touch. He needed Flintoff to stay with him at the other end.

A single took Freddie off the dreaded 'pair', and a boundary swiftly followed. But Freddie was finding it far from easy with the metronomic Pollock bowling an immaculate length, his line as straight as ever, Ntini charging in hard as usual and left-arm spinner Nicky Boje bowling over the wicket, hoping to tempt Freddie outside the leg stump to make an injudicious heave.

Freddie ultimately began to feel a whole lot better when he picked Pollock's slower ball and drove it smoothly over long on for his forty-sixth boundary six in Test-match cricket, but then an inspired spell of fizzing deliveries from Ntini beat him outside the off stump no less than eight times in three overs. The important thing, from England's point of view, was that Freddie survived with his wicket intact.

Having weathered the Ntini storm, Freddie then twice thrillingly deposited the ball over the boundary rope with well-executed hook shots when Ntini dropped short. With the experienced Graham Thorpe, he put on a priceless 114 runs before aiming a cut at part-time bowler Smith's quicker ball and snicking a top edge to the wicketkeeper. He'd made 60 and had been going well, and it was a disappointing end for Freddie to get out to an occasional off-spinner. Smith's whoops of delight as the batsman departed told their own story.

In a teatime TV interview, Freddie admitted that he'd found facing Ntini none too easy. 'I did find him difficult for a while. I'd not been playing too well out here so far, so it was nice to bat for a while and just get my head down and knuckle down.'

Flintoff's partnership with Thorpe had pushed England's lead up to 235. More importantly, it had put England very much on top for the first time in the match. And with

Thorpe going on to an unbeaten 118, and the aggressive Geraint Jones making 73, England were able to declare at 570 for 7, a total representing the biggest difference between first- and second-innings scores in England's Test history, and coming so soon after their miserable 139 on the first day. Thorpe later admitted, 'The partnerships with Freddie and Geraint were really important. They took the momentum away from South Africa.'

For England, it was an extraordinary turnaround in their match position after being shot out so quickly on the first day. Flintoff's innings of 60 contributed to only the fifth time that England had scored over 500 in the second innings of a Test. South Africa now had a target of 378 to win, a tough target which, if reached, would be the fourth-highest last-innings total to win a match in Test history.

On a dramatic and nail-biting fifth and final day, fortunes swayed first one way and then the other. England looked to have the match there for the taking when Harmison got rid of danger man Kallis just before lunch with the help of a good diving catch behind by Geraint Jones. They encountered stubborn resistance from South Africa's lower order, but with 15 overs still to bowl and just last man Steyn to come in for South Africa, the odds were good for yet another England win. Bad light had the final say, however, bringing an engrossing, epic Test to an end just as it was reaching a thrilling climax, with England tantalisingly needing to take 2 more wickets and South Africa still 88 runs short of their target.

If England had been offered the draw immediately after their poor first-innings showing, they would almost certainly have taken it, but there was no doubt which team was more relieved to have drawn the match. At the end of play, England's tired players sat together bitterly disappointed and dejected on the outfield. They'd fought so hard to turn the match around after their terrible start to the game and felt that to have been robbed of victory by the umpires' decision to offer the light to South Africa's batsmen was rough justice. Vaughan, however, couldn't complain, as the regulations concerning the light had been agreed by both sides with the officials before the series began. 'We're obviously disappointed not to have gone two–nil up,' he said, 'but after the second day we looked like losing the match in three-and-a-half days. The comeback was extraordinary.'

England's marvellous winning sequence had thus come to an end. 'It's disappointing that we haven't made it nine victories in a row,' Vaughan mused, 'but we're now unbeaten in thirteen games, which is an amazing achievement.' In fact, England ended 2004 as the only Test team to remain unbeaten throughout the year, and Freddie's big-hitting had contributed to them becoming the Test team with the fastest scoring rate that year.

'Unbelievable. Absolutely fantastic,' was Bob Willis's verdict as he reviewed the cricket year for *Sky Sports News*. The former England captain picked out Steve Harmison's devastating spell of 7 for 12 at Sabina Park, Jamaica, as the key moment that kickstarted England's wonderful year. Harmison proved, said Willis, that he wasn't a flash in the pan; he was the real deal.

Willis then paid glowing tribute to Flintoff's emergence as a world-class performer. 'Australia are going to be playing the best of the rest in October in Sydney: World Champions against the rest,' he said. 'It would be terrific if Andrew Flintoff were in that side. He would really bring something to that occasion – a bubbling all-rounder, devastating with the bat, fearsome pace with the ball, a great entertainer, brilliant slip fielder and the crowd love him.

'And the maturity that [he displayed] the previous year against the South Africans with the bat, after – it has to be said – a very long wait. [Before,] he was impetuous; he got out irresponsibly. He tried to hit every ball he received for four. All that changed. A very responsible innings changed that in 2003, and he went on and got better and better as a batsman, and thankfully his body held together.'

Freddie had bowled 37 overs in debilitating heat at Durban, and after his exertions in the field on the last day of the Durban Test he and the other weary England bowlers had just two days in which to rest before the Third Test at Newlands in Cape Town. They could have done with Michael Vaughan winning the toss to give themselves a little more respite, but crucially he lost it and they found themselves toiling away again under a merciless sun.

Fatigue was most definitely a factor as South Africa scored 441, thanks to another big 100 from Kallis. On that occasion, Freddie was England's most successful bowler, taking 4 for 79 – including the wickets of Kallis and Ntini in successive balls – in 31.1 overs. When Ntini smacked the ball high up into the air for an easy catch, he became Freddie's ninety-ninth Test victim.

Vaughan was, as ever, grateful for Freddie's willingness to run in and bowl wholeheartedly for his captain, but many – Bob Willis included – were concerned at Freddie's workload as a bowler when he also had the responsibility of batting at the important position of England's number six. 'He shouldn't be bowling 30 overs an innings,' said a critical, anxious and, as it turned out, prophetic Willis.

On the fourth day of the Test, Freddie dismissed Boeta Dippenaar with his second ball, but within an hour he suddenly pulled up awkwardly during his final spell in South Africa's second innings, grimacing with pain. He bowled the last ball of his over from a shortened run and in obvious discomfort, and then walked off the field, having completed just 4 overs that day.

By the close of play, when 5 wickets went down for 151 with Freddie out for 20, England were not only staring at defeat but also facing the prospect of losing their talismanic all-rounder from their attack for the rest of the series. Freddie was reporting soreness in his left side, and the general consensus was that he'd damaged a muscle around his ribcage, judging by the way he clutched his side. If it was indeed an intercostal injury, it might take around six weeks to heal, which meant that he'd be unable to bowl in the final two Tests. If that was the case, England would be left with the choice of either playing Freddie purely as a specialist batsman or sending him home and replacing him in the Fourth and Fifth Tests with another player.

But, as all the experts were quick to point out, without Flintoff the whole balance of the England side would be upset. Freddie was simply irreplaceable; there was no one like him in English cricket, let alone in the England touring party – which is doing no disservice to the squad's talented Paul Collingwood. Freddie's bowling would be seriously missed as an integral part of England's seam attack.

The England camp initially preferred not to say precisely what Freddie's complaint was. It was too soon for a diagnosis without taking an X-ray, but the subsequent summoning of Kevin Pietersen as an addition to the One-Day squad was an indication that Freddie was indeed struggling with his fitness.

When Freddie batted in the second innings as England fought to avoid defeat in the Third Test, he showed no obvious signs of discomfort but was out cheaply as England finally succumbed by 196 runs. In defeat, the only silver lining for Freddie was that there was now a period of seven days before the next Test in which to rest his body, try to recuperate and – if necessary – get treatment for his injury, which was diagnosed as a grade-one tear of an oblique muscle at the bottom of the ribcage.

Inevitably after this bulletin was released, there was renewed debate as to whether Freddie had been overbowled by his captain, and this persisted for the next few days. It was a hot topic, particularly when the statistics showed that Freddie had sent down 49.1 overs in the game, more than any England bowler and 22 more than Simon Jones, to whom Vaughan sometimes seemed reluctant to toss the ball. Duncan Fletcher, however, pointed out, 'These kind of injuries can come from anything. Sometimes it comes from not bowling, and sometimes it comes from too much bowling. [Freddie's] had quite a lot of bowling, but it's not all in one big spell; he's been bowling around 15 overs a day, and this series has been going on for three weeks now.'

As the team moved on to Johannesburg, discussion of Freddie's bowling role in the team continued among ex-players, cricket correspondents, the travelling Barmy Army and England cricket followers back home. There was no doubt that England had gone into the series with the idea of using Freddie in short bursts with a view to his bowling perhaps twelve to fifteen overs a day, but that plan had partly depended on Harmison firing on all cylinders, as had been hoped of the man who had gone into the series as the world's number-one bowler. Harmison, however, had disappointingly fallen well short of the high standards he had set himself during 2004 and his radar was frequently askew as he struggled for line and length. And, with Harmison misfiring, Vaughan tended to turn to Freddie either when he needed his control and economical overs to rein back the South African scoring or when he was looking to take a much-needed wicket.

As each day passed in the run-up to the Fourth Test, reports about the all-rounder's chances of playing at least a major part in the game as a bowler became more encouraging, even though Freddie conspicuously confined his net practice to batting only.

Freddie eventually surfaced as a bowler only on the day before the Test was due to start, and then proceeded to bowl a mere 20 balls at one stump at three-quarter pace. He began cautiously, gradually increasing his pace until the ball was carrying through at chest height to Geraint Jones, standing well back. It hardly seemed ideal preparation for a five-day Test, but all the indications were that he would play at the magnificent Wanderers Stadium and that he would bowl. And England desperately needed him.

Tellingly, the statistics as England went into the Fourth Test showed that Freddie was their most successful bowler in the Test series thus far with 14 wickets, a fact to which Vaughan alluded in his pre-match interviews on the eve of the game. The captain defended his decision to bowl Freddie as much as he had, instead of the fresher Simon Jones, by saying that he'd been anxious to delay South Africa's declaration at Cape Town by a potentially vital few minutes and that Freddie was the man to help him do it. 'Sometimes,' he added, 'it's hard to get the ball out of his hands.' He was, however, full of praise for

Freddie's efforts with the ball. 'He's bowled really, really well for us. He's probably been our best bowler, with Matthew Hoggard, and he's going to play a huge part for us in the next two weeks if we're going to win the series.'

Vaughan was also quick to play down the seriousness of Freddie's side strain. 'You're always a bit wary about people coming back from slight injuries,' he said, 'but you've got to realise it's only a little injury. We're very, very confident he'll come through the game, and get through the two games going into the One-Dayers as well. We'll just have to see. We've got a decent attack, and Freddie's been the pinnacle point of that attack in this series. We expect him to play a full part here.'

Fortunately for Freddie, Vaughan won the toss and chose to bat, which gave his star all-rounder another vital two days of rest from bowling. England proceeded to post a total of 411 for 8 – thanks mainly to 147 from Strauss – on two rain-interrupted days before declaring before the start of the third morning's play.

After England took the field, all eyes were on Freddie to see how he would fare when he was eventually called up to bowl, but, when he took the ball, if he was feeling the strain, he didn't show it. He was soon settling into his rhythm, bowling in the mid-eighties mph, and had the satisfaction of removing Boeta Dippenaar for a duck. It was just as well for England that Freddie was operating efficiently, because he was asked to get through 30.1 overs as South Africa fought back hard to get a first-innings lead of 8.

South Africa were led by Herschelle Gibbs, who returned to form with a fine century, but he was lucky to survive in Freddie's last over of the third day. Drawn into a push outside the off stump, Gibbs edged what would have been a fairly straightforward catch for Marcus Trescothick at first slip had Geraint Jones not plunged across him with a despairing dive. The luckless bowler was halfway into a celebratory leap when he saw to his anguish the keeper spill the chance. It proved to be a costly miss, as Gibbs went on to make 161 next day.

The match was finely balanced until the fifth day, which belonged to Matthew Hoggard and, in the morning, to Marcus Trescothick. First the left-handed opener played beautifully and powerfully to make a magnificent 180, which set up a declaration, leaving South Africa to make 325 to win in 68 overs. Hoggard then destroyed their long batting line-up by taking 7 for 61.

But Hoggard's wasn't just a one-man show with the ball. The South Africans went into tea on 98 for 5, and it was after the interval that a fired-up Freddie gave Hoggard the back-up he and England needed. Vaughan asked Freddie to give it everything he had and to bowl as fast as he could, and Freddie responded by cranking up his pace to 90mph.

Later, when Vaughan had to leave the field briefly for some running repairs, and when Hoggard required a rest, Freddie went up to acting captain Trescothick and requested that he be given the ball. Showing great strength and energy for someone who was supposed to be bowling within himself, Freddie proceeded to produce a terrific spell, the quickest of the match. One particular moment that exemplified his willingness, spirit and commitment occurred when Freddie followed through to field a ball off his own bowling, throwing himself full-length and bone-jarringly to the ground to reach the ball with an outstretched hand.

Freddie's determination and aggression gave England a boost as the overs began to slip away and it became a race against time. First he roughed up Shaun Pollock and hit him on the helmet, the ball ricocheting back out to midwicket. Then he followed up by pushing Pollock back and still further back before producing a snorter that squared up the South African all-rounder and induced a snick to Jones, behind the wicket.

After Makhaya Ntini had held up England for a while, it was Freddie who finally trapped the fast bowler LBW to bring last man Dale Steyn to the wicket to join Graeme Smith. The South African captain had come in down the order after suffering mild concussion from a blow on the temple from a ball during fielding practice, and it was a brave gesture by him to bat at all against medical advice.

Smith also showed no little skill in farming the bowling, even keeping the strike away from his inexperienced number eleven by outrageously scampering byes when deliveries from the fast bowlers flew straight through to the keeper's gloves.

For Freddie and England, there came one agonising

moment with the final pair together when he lured Smith into flashing a drive to Anderson at deep point. The ball flew at catchable height, but the chance went down. Freddie isn't usually one to show his frustration outwardly at a catch dropped off his bowling, but this occasion – when it would have been all over if Anderson had clung on – was different and a pained look of utter anguish crossed his face.

How costly that miss might be was emphasised when Smith and Steyn managed to put on 31. Fortunately for England, however, Hoggard summoned up one more effort to have Steyn caught behind to give England a truly stunning victory by 77 runs with just 8.3 overs in hand.

The exuberance of the England players' on-pitch celebrations indicated that they knew this performance had been very special. Freddie, who was pictured grinning broadly and brandishing a stump, might have had a below-par game with the bat, twice getting out to poor shots, but he'd once again shown his great all-round value to the team. Hoggard was the hero, of course, but Freddie had taken 2 for 59 in his 16 overs and had sent down a total of 46.1 overs in the match – not bad for a fast bowler nursing a side injury and, as it later transpired, secretly braving the pain of a recurrence of his long-standing ankle problem.

Each Test in the series had stretched to five days, and the statistics showed that by the end of the Fourth Test Freddie had bowled a series total of 169.2 overs – one more than Hoggard, who repeatedly (and justifiably) wins plaudits from ex-players, his peers, cricket writers, commentators and supporters for his willingness to keep running in all day for his captain.

The efforts of the two workhorses weren't lost on anyone. David Morgan, chairman of the England and Wales Cricket Board, commented, 'I wouldn't like to see this kind of schedule repeated, because I think it's unfair on the players. Of course, it can't be ideal for Matthew Hoggard or Andrew Flintoff to have only three days off after the kind of match we had at the Wanderers. Playing Test after Test must be extremely difficult.' Fortunately for the welfare of the likes of Andrew Flintoff and others who are rarely out of the game, a review of the international cricket calendar is under way.

Less than forty-eight hours after England's remarkable win at the Wanderers, the general euphoria of such an unlikely victory was tempered by fresh fears surfacing about Freddie's long-term fitness. Once again the Flintoff scare stories making the back-page headlines concerned his persistent ankle injury after England physio Kirk Russell revealed that for the past two Tests Freddie had been suffering from a recurrence of a problem with a bone spur in his left heel. It was the same heel problem that had developed in the summer of 2004 after three Tests against New Zealand which resulted in his not bowling again for England for six weeks. The revelation made his monumental workload in Johannesburg and Cape Town seem all the more remarkable and courageous.

Then, as now, injections had masked the problem and allowed him to return to action, but injections were always a temporary solution, not a cure. Now an operation to cure the chronic complaint was beckoning – which posed the question nervously asked by everyone with England's cricket fortunes at heart: What sort of condition would Andrew Flintoff be in to face the Aussies in the battle for the Ashes in the summer? And there were doom-mongers who questioned whether or not he'd be fit to face the Aussies at all in the summer. Informed speculation not officially confirmed prior to the Fifth Test was that he would miss the One-Day Internationals against South Africa and was likely to fly home as soon as the Test series was over to undergo an operation to sort out his long-standing problem once and for all.

Since it was Bangladesh – one of the lesser powers in world cricket – who England would be hosting during the first part of the 2005 English summer, it was judged that there would be time and opportunity for Freddie to have the surgery and be back to full fitness by the time the Ashes Tests began in July.

Shaun Pollock, who underwent a similar operation to cure the same sort of problem as Flintoff, suggested that Freddie take the opportunity to get his ankle fixed once the Test series against South Africa was over. 'If he was to have the operation done straight away, then by the time the Ashes Tests came along, he'd be all right.' Speaking from experience, he reckoned that recuperation would take Freddie four to five months, six weeks of which Freddie would spend with his ankle in plaster, followed by plenty of time in the pool and gym, working back to fitness.

With such a congested international calendar, having the operation now seemed to make sense – particularly to former South African pace bowler Allan Donald, who noted poignantly that he'd kept having to have injection after injection to keep him going because the international schedule was too busy to allow him to bow out temporarily and have a similar operation.

History showed that there was no reason to doubt that such an operation wouldn't cure Freddie's problem, which was a common complaint among fast bowlers, caused by bones rubbing together and aggravated by continually banging the left foot down in the footholds during deliveries. What was encouraging for Freddie was that Shaun Pollock, his fellow South African Lance Klusener and Australia's Glenn McGrath had all had similar corrective surgery and gone on to perform once again at cricket's highest level. However, history also showed that, being such a big man, Flintoff tended to take longer to get over such injuries than other professional cricketers. It was David Gower who summed up every English cricket fan's fears when he said, 'It would be the greatest shame of all time if Flintoff's not fit to play against Australia in the Ashes.'

First, however, there was a Fifth Test at Centurion for Freddie to gear himself up for, with England needing at least a draw to make history and clinch the series.

With Harmison nursing an injured calf, Ashley Giles still

inconvenienced with his broken thumb and Simon Jones having suffered back spasms on tour, the sight of Andrew Flintoff at practice for the Fifth Test with support splints on either side of his left ankle didn't bode well for England's chances in the final Test in Pretoria. However, thanks to a cortisone injection, Freddie was in the side and would play his part.

The first day of the Test was washed out by rain, and when Michael Vaughan won the toss on the second day he had no hesitation in putting South Africa in on the greenest, grassiest of wickets anyone could remember. It was the sort of track that looked ideal for seam bowling, but Harmison was still having trouble with his radar (although he had two catches dropped off him) and Hoggard wasn't at his best. England had a poor morning with the new ball on a wicket that should have given them plenty of assistance.

It was left to Freddie to come to England's rescue, first by putting a hold on the South Africans' advance by breaking the opening partnership, and then by turning the game around with two wickets in three balls soon after tea.

South Africa appeared to be batting their way to a big score when, for the umpteenth time since he became captain, Vaughan turned to Freddie to get him a wicket and to bring some much-needed control to the England attack. Freddie duly obliged in his very first over by luring Herschelle Gibbs forward outside the off stump to give a thin edge through to the wicketkeeper. It moved Allan Donald to say to millions of watching TV viewers, '[Freddie's] broken partnerships throughout the series, almost at will. He's been a special player in this series.'

However, on a wicket where England might have hoped to bowl out the opposition for 150, the South Africans still went into lunch well placed at 114 for 1 and handily placed at tea on 196 for 4, even though Freddie had dismissed Kallis with one of the best balls of the series: a fast yorker with a hint of swing that sent Kallis's off stump flying out of the ground after he'd made just 8.

After tea, Freddie made sure that the game swung dramatically England's way. First, he drew Graeme Smith into a wide, expansive drive that ended up in the hands of Marcus Trescothick at slip. Two balls later, he sent Pollock's middle stump flying for yards when the batsman got a thick inside edge on to his wicket. Freddie's spell yielded just 12 runs for his 2 wickets and he'd rarely bowled better in his Test career. He finished the innings with figures of 19 overs, 6 maidens and 4 wickets for 44 runs. His victims were four batsmen who had scored forty Test-match 100s between them.

Replying to South Africa's 247, England were once again in some trouble at 114 for 4 when Freddie came out to bat. And rarely can he have walked to the middle in such threatening circumstances, not just from the prospect of facing a fired-up Ntini and a bristling, verbally hostile Andre Nel but from the most violent of storms about to engulf Centurion.

When Freddie reached the crease, the ground was in semi-darkness below threatening dark clouds, which were alarmingly pierced periodically by forked lightning flashing behind the stands. Thunder rumbled all around and a fierce wind threatened to tear the team flags from their poles. In such gloom the umpires had no option but to take off the players. Freddie hadn't even had time to take guard.

The first hour next morning was crucial and, if South Africa were to have any sniff of a chance of winning the match and squaring the series, they needed to bowl England out before lunch. With Thorpe scrapping it out at the other end, Freddie got his head down and concentrated on keeping his wicket intact, occupying the crease and patiently playing himself into form.

The South African bowlers – especially Andre Nel – came hard at the batsmen, and the Flintoff–Nel confrontation was certainly one that the spectators were hotly anticipating. The England fans were longing for Freddie to batter Nel out of the ground in answer to the volatile fast bowler's trademark icy stares and glares, while the South African supporters were looking forward to the controversial Nel unleashing his full repertoire of noisy, belligerent histrionics and getting right up Freddie's nose.

In the event, the contest between the two was tough but not explosive. Never at a loss for a harsh word to say to any batsman, Nel had almost overstepped the mark with his venomous verbals the previous day and now restricted himself to grimacing and eyeballing them. Freddie, meanwhile, was reining in his natural instincts with the bat and concentrating on occupying the crease and not taking any risks. It took him 56 balls to advance from 10 to 20, and a total of 110 balls to reach 30. His 50 came up in 123 balls and took 169 minutes, making it the slowest of his fourteen Test half-centuries. For such a natural strokeplayer, it was a thoroughly responsible knock, showing just the kind of disciplined approach England required.

With Grahame Thorpe, Freddie put on 141 before he was out for 77, a total that included a hook off Ntini that cleared the rope at square leg. It was Freddie's fiftieth six in Tests, and as it soared over the boundary he joined an elite group, becoming only the fifteenth player to reach that big-hitting half-century milestone in Test-match history.

Thanks to a gritty 86 from Thorpe, England built a lead of 109 and had a chance to put the South African batsmen under pressure before the close of play on the fourth day. Buoyed by his endeavours with the bat, and with Harmison still suffering from a sore calf, Freddie was given the new ball in preference to his friend and repaid Vaughan's faith in him by bowling fast to a perfect line and length, having Gibbs caught behind the wicket and then ripping out Hall's off stump, 2 wickets that put England well on top. His day's efforts with bat and ball earned the headline FLINTOFF'S ALL-ROUND BRILLIANCE GIVES HOPE OF VICTORY in *The Times*, while the *Daily Mail* boldly hailed him as 'the history man', adding: 'Fantastic Fred ensures forty-year wait for series triumph will end.'

On another fluctuating final day, South Africa eventually set

England a target of 182 to win at 4.2 an over and there were alarm bells ringing when they slumped to 20 for 3. But a watchful Vaughan, another sixty-nine minutes of defiance from Thorpe and some dogged defence from Freddie made sure that all the hard work wouldn't be undone. The Barmy Army and other England fans, watching from the grass embankments of Centurion's Supersport Park, cheered every run and every blocked ball as England inched ever nearer to safety.

Fittingly, after a magnificent all-round performance, Freddie was there at the end on 14 not out, batting with his captain, to see the game through to the series-clinching draw. He left the field grinning broadly and was mobbed by England supporters chanting, 'Bring on the Aussies', as he and Vaughan made their way up the long flight of steps to the pavilion.

If this was to be Freddie's last hurrah on a cricket field for England for six months, then he'd signed off with a big final effort, a massively influential contribution with both bat and ball. England had won their fourth Test series in a row, and after forty years without success they had indeed made history on South African soil.

Freddie finished the series with two important half-centuries as his main contributions with the bat, although his average of 28.37 was below par for the standards he'd set himself the previous year. However, he was top of England's bowling averages, with 23wickets at 24.95 apiece – better than Ntini's average for the series. Only Hoggard, with 26, took more wickets for England. Significantly, Freddie bowled 201.2

overs, more than any other England bowler and more than twice as many as Jacques Kallis.

Immediately after the game, Freddie divulged cricket's worst-kept secret: that he would be flying home to see a specialist in England straight away to fix an early date for surgery and devise a strict recuperation programme, with the Ashes in mind. If he had the operation immediately, his ankle would be out of plaster in time for his wedding to Rachael in March.

Having had to fly home from the South African tour in 2000 with a stress fracture in his foot, it was another crushing disappointment for the all-rounder to be boarding an early plane once again. He was sad to miss the One-Day Internationals against South Africa, but after missing out on the last two battles for the Ashes he saw it as a chance to get into peak condition for a third opportunity.

Freddie's departure dealt a severe blow to England's One-Day squad, seriously unbalancing the side, and his economical bowling and fast scoring would be sadly missed. It could have been argued that, on recent performances, Freddie was the best One-Day player in the world; in his last thirty One-Day Internationals he had scored 1,201 runs at an average of 57.19 and taken 40 wickets at 18.60 apiece.

Freddie left for home with all good wishes from his teammates – and, indeed, from cricket fans everywhere – and with an unexpected but touchingly warm send-off from Graeme Smith. The tough South African captain used a column in the *Daily Telegraph* to convey how disappointed he was to see Freddie returning home. 'He's a fantastic competitor and an equally fantastic guy. Staying in the same hotel as England was a pleasure with Freddie around and I'm pleased to say we had a couple of beers together after play and reminded ourselves that there is life outside cricket. Good luck with the op, Fred.'

Arriving back in Manchester on Thursday, 27 January less than thirty hours after England had sealed their historic series victory, Freddie was upbeat about being ready for the Aussies. 'That's five months away, so I've got a long time. I've never played yet in a Test match against Australia, so hopefully by the time they come over I'll be in peak condition. It will also give me a chance to work at my game while I'm recovering and get myself in great shape for when they come to contest the Ashes.

'There's a belief in the camp. We played in South Africa and won two–one, not playing by any means to our potential, so we've got a good chance.'

At around the same time that Freddie's plane was touching down at Manchester, Graham Thorpe was arriving back at Heathrow and looking ahead to the summer, although he was slightly more cautious about England's chances. 'We know exactly where we have to improve. We have to bat a lot better, with much more strength and depth than we did on this tour, and our bowling has to be more consistent as well. But that doesn't take away from our achievement out in South Africa. It's just that, if you want to do well against Australia, everything has to be perfect and in order. If we don't play to our potential, we'll get a hiding.'

Despite the explosive heroics of Kevin Pietersen in the One-Day Internationals against South Africa, with three stunning 100s full of Flintoff-style blows, his eye-catching performances couldn't disguise the fact that England struggled with both bat and ball in Freddie's absence. In his end-of-series report, Richard Hobson, the One-Day cricket correspondent for *The Times*, went as far as to say, 'Despite the stellar emergence of Kevin Pietersen, any England team that does not include Andrew Flintoff remains in the second tier of the international game. With him, as they showed in knocking Australia out of the ICC Champions Trophy at Edgbaston five months ago, England are strong enough to beat any opposition on any given day.'

The bald statistics showed that, since the 2003 World Cup, England had won seventeen and lost six One-Day Internationals when Freddie was playing. Without him, the record was very different: five wins, seven losses and one tie. If the meaningless victory over weakened Zimbabwe was discounted, England's record was just one win from nine games when Freddie was missing from the team.

CHAPTER 14

Little Urn

'Bring on the Aussies!'

CHANT FROM ENGLAND'S BARMY ARMY AT SUPERSPORT PARK, CENTURION, AFTER ENGLAND WON THE 2004–5 TEST SERIES AGAINST SOUTH AFRICA

Nothing excites an England cricket fan more than the prospect of beating Australia. And, while the win over South Africa was a notable achievement, the players themselves knew that the biggest test of their worth as a team was to come in 2005 when Australia, the current world champions, arrived in England.

No one was looking forward to the Ashes more than Andrew Flintoff. He had never played a Test match against Australia, a strange statistic considering that he was first capped by England as a twenty-year-old, that he was now twenty-eight years of age and that, in the intervening years, he had played forty-five times for his country at Test level, including taking part in three series against South Africa.

His lack of participation in Tests between the game's

greatest international rivals was a reflection of his stuttering start as an international cricketer and of how he has been plagued by injuries during his career.

The upside of this odd statistic was that Freddie was not one of the England cricketers who knew what it was like to lose Test series after Test series to the Aussies, as was the case with many of England's recent stalwarts like Alec Stewart, Darren Gough and Nasser Hussain, who played in five of the eight series since England had last held the Ashes in 1987.

Some rated this current Australian side as the best cricket team ever, better even than Bradman's magnificent 1948 Australians. Ricky Ponting's men had steamrollered all opponents in recent years, and they had mostly done it with flair and style, scoring so quickly that they changed the tempo of Test cricket and raised it to a new level.

But, given that he was fit, challenging for the Ashes in 2005 against England's old enemy would be a new experience for Freddie, as it would be for other England players like Andrew Strauss, Geraint Jones, Ian Bell and Kevin Pietersen who had also yet to play against Australia. Steve Harmison, too, had had very limited experience of Test cricket against the Aussies, and by 2005 he was a very different bowler from the one they had confronted previously.

So important had Freddie now become to the England team that most experts agreed that England had little chance of winning back the Ashes, or even competing with Australia, unless he was 100 per cent fit when the two teams assembled for the First Test beginning at Lord's on 21 July and, most importantly, stayed fit throughout the series.

It's no exaggeration to say that, if Freddie was firing with bat and ball and playing well, then England were usually playing good cricket and having a decent day. The downside was that the weight of expectation upon him could hardly have been heavier. 'There are times when I have felt the pressure,' he said, 'but at the moment I play cricket the only way I can. I enjoy hitting the ball, I enjoy trying to bowl fast and that is what I do, then I go home in the evenings, spend time with the missus and the baby and that relieves everything.'

It wasn't just his abilities on the field as an all-rounder that had given England an edge. His very presence in the side allowed the selectors and the captain to pick another spinner or seamer, or even play another batsman. He was giving them options, as well as providing the safest pair of hands at slip.

His workload as a bowler remained a talking point and would continue to be so on his return to action. The other major debate about Freddie's role in the side was whether he should bat at number six or at number seven where some felt he might have greater licence to play his wonderful array of attacking shots.

Around this time, there was talk, too, of Freddie as a future England captain. He had captained England in warm-up games and many believed he would make a good fist of the job as skipper. But, in the interests of the side, purely on a performance level it would be asking a very great deal of him to bowl long spells, bat in the middle order and catch everything at slip, as well as having the burden of captaincy.

But, above all, he is that priceless commodity for any cricket team – the all-rounder who is genuinely batsman *and* bowler, two players rolled into one. And as a bowler he can play two roles, either coming on as the enforcer to bowl fast to shake up the opposition and get a wicket or two, or to use his control to frustrate the batsmen and keep the run rate in check. Since he became a Sky Sports commentator, Nasser Hussain has frequently been effusive about Freddie's ability to sit in and bowl to a plan for his captain. He often asked Freddie to do so, and Michael Vaughan does the same.

In these days of computerised analysis by international coaches of every ball bowled and every shot played, it does not take long for information about a player to get around the international circuit – and the Australians had been taking Flintoff very seriously, especially since his exploits in 2004. Australia's world-beating team might not have come up against Freddie except in a handful of One-Day Internationals, but they knew the effect he could have if he got up a head of steam with the ball in his hand and the way he could change a game with his batting.

'He's a genuine match-winner. And he would walk into the Australian team,' said Shane Warne in a review of the 2004 season for *The Times*. Warne was perhaps better placed than many of his Aussie teammates in his assessment of Flintoff because he had spent Freddie's golden summer in England, captaining Hampshire.

Warne pointed out that Freddie had played Bangladesh, Sri Lanka, West Indies home and away and a New Zealand team minus Shane Bond, the Kiwis' best strike bowler. Freddie's recent record was indeed highly impressive, said Warne, and showed that if teams bowled badly at him then he would destroy them. But he stressed that South Africa and Australia would be far sterner tests.

'Flintoff has the personality to be "the man",' wrote Warne, 'and I think he gets off on that. He isn't pretending to be a character. And he gets the odd break because of his confidence and self-belief,' Warne added, possibly recalling Freddie's mis-hit six which sailed over the wicketkeeper's head and over the boundary rope when he top-edged a hook aimed at a fast ball from Brett Lee when England beat Australia by 6 wickets in their ICC Champions Trophy semi-final match in 2004. 'It is no coincidence,' continued Warne. 'Players who change games are the ones who back themselves and have an aura that sends signals to the opposition.'

Freddie's confrontation with master spinner Warne, the world's leading wicket-taker, was a contest which cricket fans both in England and Down Under had been looking forward to with relish for a year or two. Warne had never been easy to hit, but Freddie possessed the character and the strokes with which to attack the leg spinner. It would be an intriguing confrontation.

With Freddie to the fore, most experts agreed that England had to play aggressively if they were to get at the Australians. They could not afford to sit back and wait for things to happen. Not since Ian Botham was in his pomp two decades earlier had England possessed a player who mentally put one over the Australians. Australian batsmen like to win the mental battle by imposing themselves on the opposition bowlers and bullying them – which again was why a fit Freddie was so crucial. He was England's talisman, capable of whistling a 90mph past Ricky Ponting's nose or climbing into Brett Lee, one of the quickest bowlers in the world, with the bat.

Australians respect players who stand up to them and, if he was firing on all cylinders, it was felt Freddie was big enough in every sense to come at them. At six feet four and weighing over sixteen stone, he can be an intimidating figure for a batsman as he runs in to bowl. He's a key player who would be encouraged to play his way and express himself.

Prior to the Ashes battle of 2005, there was perhaps no more meaningful accolade given to Freddie than that by a former Australian star who played the game as hard as anyone – Rod Marsh.

The former wicketkeeper-batsman predicted in an interview for BBC World Service that the battle for the Ashes could be a tight series. He said, 'England have got themselves into some terrible fixes but manage to get out and win games just like Australia have done. Australia have been in some horrible fixes but all of a sudden Gilchrist comes in and in an hour changes a game.

'There are few people who do that as well – Flintoff springs to mind. He is a fine cricketer – he hits the ball as hard as anyone and he can bowl and he can catch.

'He's right up there as far as ability is concerned and he's got a very good attitude to the game.'

From the moment he walks on to the field to bat, Freddie sends out a message of intent to the opposition. He purposefully strides to the crease carrying his helmet in one hand like a Roman gladiator entering the Coliseum. He's so big and tall that the bat in his other hand almost looks like a toothpick.

In his eagerness to get out to the middle, Freddie invariably passes the outgoing batsman almost halfway to the wicket, which signals to the bowlers that he can't wait to get out there and get at them. Freddie's early entrance on to the playing arena can be harsh on the outgoing batsman. Applause for a good innings played switches to cheers of anticipation from the crowd for the first sighting of Freddie emerging from the pavilion. He draws the applause away from the outgoing batsman.

Nasser Hussain is just one of many who believe that Freddie has it in him to become one of the greatest all-rounders of all time. But, if the game's administrators continue to ask so much of the players, the days of the outstanding all-rounders enjoying long careers at the top level may soon be over. Their spirit might be willing, but their bodies simply won't be able to last the pace.

Not so long ago, Test cricket boasted some of the best all-rounders ever to play the game: Richard Hadlee and Chris Cairns for New Zealand, Imran Khan and Wasim Akram for Pakistan, Ian Botham for England, and Kapil Dev for India. All bowled fast, made big runs for their countries and enjoyed prolonged careers. But that was before international teams were asked to play the exhausting amount of cricket they do today – a typical English summer comprises seven Tests and thirteen One-Day matches and England are expected to play a similar amount of games away from home in return.

In South Africa in the winter of 2004–5, Andrew Flintoff revealed that, in his career, he had needed a total of around twenty injections in his arms, back and ankle to keep pushing himself through the pain barrier in summers past. Down the years, he's played at various times in a corset to help his back and, more recently, with splints in his boot to ease the pain in his ankle.

As long ago as 2000 in Lahore, before he really established himself as an England Test player, he admitted, 'I've always regarded myself as a batting all-rounder, and my target for a long time has been to bat number four or five in the Test team.' It is unrealistic to expect him to bowl 30 overs an innings if he is to reach that target. But if, like Jacques Kallis, in years to come he becomes a batsman who occasionally bowls, he will still rank as one of cricket's biggest attractions for the way he strikes the ball vast distances and with a smile on his face.

'My batting philosophy has always been: "If it's there, then hit it",' he said recently. 'It's something that I just have to do. Sometimes I choose the wrong ball and the result is usually a disaster. But shot selection is something that improves with time and experience. If you try to score off every ball then you can't just push it back or leave it, and that can cause problems.

'But for me, the sweetest feeling has always been hitting the ball straight back over the bowler's head for six. It doesn't matter how many times you do it, it always feels great.'

Discounting Alec Stewart, who was world class as a wicketkeeper-batsman, England had not had an all-rounder of the highest class since Ian Botham retired. Every time an England cricketer showed signs of being able to bat and bowl at medium pace or above, the dreaded question was always asked: 'Is this the new Botham?' The constant comparison was a millstone around the necks of the likes of Phil DeFreitas, David Capel, Chris Lewis and Dominic Cork who all suffered from overblown expectations.

The word is overused, but Botham qualifies as a legend, and Freddie knows as well as anyone that he was unique. 'People want an all-rounder, I know that,' Freddie said recently. 'We had Ian Botham, who was probably our best-ever cricketer and everyone after him has been labelled as the next one. But you're never going to get another Botham. I'm just trying to make my way. I work hard and play as I play.'

Suffice to say that Botham has long been an admirer of Freddie's and they enjoy a good relationship. Botham has given him excellent encouragement and advice, and he believed Freddie had the character and the game to carry the fight to the Australians. Botham has been as pleased as anyone at Andrew's progress and says of Freddie, 'He's a breath of fresh air in the game.'

Ominously for the world's bowlers, Freddie believes it will be several years before he reaches his peak. 'Some of the best batters in the world probably peaked at thirty or thirty-one, so I have got a bit in me yet,' he says. 'As a batter I am hoping I am getting better and better and when I get to thirty-three I hope I will be firing on all cylinders.'

On a February morning in 2005 when England's One-Day bowlers were being battered for more than 300 runs in 50 overs under cloudless skies in South Africa, England cricket fans at least had something to feel cheerful about – the news that was emanating from the unlikely source of the racecourse at Carlisle.

Among interested observers at the Carlisle race meeting on 9 February was the unmistakeable figure of Andrew Flintoff, suitably dressed for the occasion in wax jacket and flat cap, and walking about with the aid of crutches. The much-talked-about operation on his ankle was now behind him, and ahead of him was a strict, disciplined return-to-fitness regime, which he was taking seriously enough even to cancel his honeymoon in case it interrupted such a carefully structured rehabilitation programme.

Freddie was confident enough of the outcome to promise, 'I'll get fit for the Ashes. It's something I'm really looking forward to, and I can't wait.

'I had the operation a week last Sunday and it went fine,' he said cheerfully. 'The spur on the back of my ankle was slightly bigger than they thought, but that is not a major thing. So, hopefully, I will be back playing in three or four months. I can't wait, to be honest. I have never played a Test match against Australia and I am desperate to do that. They are the best team in the world and I want to test myself against the best. It's going to be the biggest summer of my life.'

It was an upbeat bulletin from Freddie and its message was lapped up by England cricket fans. At the Carlisle races, there were words aplenty from well-wishers and it prompted the question as to how he was coping with his iconic status within the game. 'I'm the same bloke I was when I was eighteen, except I'm just enjoying my cricket a bit more now,' he said. 'By no means do I regard myself as a celebrity.'

While Freddie was optimistically talking up his fitness prospects for the Ashes before hobbling off to a private box to watch the races, there was another Flintoff catching the eye at Carlisle, and this one appeared anything but lame – a horse named after the cricketer which was running in the HBLB 'Junior' Standard Open National Hunt Flat Race. The four-year-old gelding, in which Freddie has a half-share, looked to be going well but came in at 12–1, three-and-a-half lengths behind 40–1 shot Sotovik in the bumper. Freddie was far from dejected, however, and said afterwards, 'He's run a really good race on only his second start.'

It transpired that Freddie's half-share in Flintoff the horse was an early wedding present from his good friend Paul Beck whose company LBM sponsors Lancashire County Cricket Club and also trainer Richard Guest's yard.

It was Paul Beck who had originally introduced Freddie to racing with a day out at Nottingham a few years before, and Freddie had readily agreed when Beck asked if he would mind a horse being named after him. 'It escalated from there,' Freddie explained. 'About three weeks ago I was in Johannesburg and the phone went and it was Paul saying, "Fill the forms in, this is your wedding present. Half the horse."

'I'm getting quite involved, to be honest. I really enjoy it and it is a bit of a release from what I do. It is a bit of a social day, too, but I am not much of a punter. I don't mind spending money but one of the things I hate is losing. I enjoy the days out and at some point I want to expand – obviously finances depending. It is something I am interested in – my missus's grandfather Terry had Piccolo, so he is into horses, and it is something I am going to get into. But I will probably wait until my playing career is over, then I can go and see the horses.'

While watching the four-legged Flintoff flying around the Carlisle course, Freddie had an ear out for events in South

Africa and made time to text a message of congratulations to Kevin Pietersen on his blistering 100s in the One-Day Internationals. He told Pietersen how much he was looking forward to batting with him in the summer and the two of them doing some damage together.

Immediately after Freddie had undergone surgery, he headed down to London to meet up with his good friend David English for a quiet meal. 'I got a telephone call from Freddie,' said David, 'in which he told me, "I'm just going in for my operation so I can't talk to you for a couple of hours but I'll call you when I get out." He came out of the op and called me, as he said he would, and asked if we could have a quiet evening together and he would bring Rob Key along.

'So I met up with him that evening, and he came in with his crutches and a huge club foot after the op and we had a glass of wine and bit of a chat and I asked him how the ankle was. "It's fine, don't worry about that," he said, clearly wanting to get on with life and talk about something else.

'He's still the lovely bloke he was when I first met him. His wife Rachael and becoming a father to little Holly are the best things that ever happened to him. Meeting Rachael was a big thing, but being a dad has made him more considered and controlled in his cricket as well.

'When you're a single man you live for the moment, don't you? But he now knows there's something else apart from cricket that's more important in his life. So therefore he enjoys his cricket and takes it more seriously, but in his own exuberant way, knowing he's got a lovely wife and a lovely little daughter to go home to.'

How different his life is now from the Andrew Flintoff who lived untidily in a flat with some mates, ate everything that was put in front of him and was in danger of squandering his natural gifts due to a lackadaisical lifestyle. Now, instead of a messy flat in central Manchester, he comes home to a fabulous home in Cheshire where a beautiful wife and baby daughter and his two boxer dogs, Arnold and Fred, treasure the moments he is around before he takes off on another cricketing journey.

His role as husband and father is clearly identified now. Similarly, his role in the England team had been clearly identified to him and he felt comfortable with it. Freddie himself summed it all up by saying, 'Maybe all the pieces of the jigsaw have always been there in the box. But now it feels like they are fitting together.'

On 5 March 2005, Freddie and Rachael were married in London and their reception for family members and a hundred friends was held, fittingly, at 30 Pavilion Road in Knightsbridge. Freddie sported a crew cut for his big day, a legacy of some hi-jinx during his stag weekend in Budapest where all but a tuft of his hair was shaved off by his pals.

Forgoing a honeymoon in order not to disrupt his rehabilitation, Freddie was soon back under the watchful eye of physio Dave Roberts. Three times a week he was to be found in the hydrotherapy pool at the £7 million academy of

Premiership football club Blackburn Rovers where recuperative sessions featured elements of yoga and Pilates, overseen by Rhiannon Jones, a specialist in posture and balance.

The good news for Lancashire was that Freddie was given clearance by the England and Wales Cricket Board to start the season with his county rather than in the two-Test series against Bangladesh. 'The plan is that Freddie will start off playing just as a batsman and then gradually build up bowling a few overs,' said Mike Watkinson, Lancashire's director of cricket. 'When he bowls and how much will be up to him and how he feels.'

One thing was for sure. Freddie definitely felt like bowling at some Aussies.

CHAPTER 15

A True Sportsman

'It will go down as one of the great moments in sportsmanship. He could have hugged his mates and celebrated but he chose to put his arm around me.'

BRETT LEE ON FREDDIE'S CONSOLING GESTURE AT THE END OF THE SECOND ENGLAND–AUSTRALIA TEST AT EDGBASTON, 2005

If any England cricket fan had seen Andrew Flintoff hobbling along the streets of Prague accompanied by a few of his teammates on his stag weekend in January 2005, they wouldn't have given much for his chances of batting and bowling England to victory in the Ashes series just a few months away.

And yet, by the end of the summer, Freddie was a national hero, his glorious exploits winning him acclaim on the front and back pages of every newspaper in the land.

In a truly thrilling sequence of matches rated as the greatest ever Test series, Freddie produced a string of outstanding performances with both bat and ball, which went a very long way to England wresting back the Ashes from Australia after sixteeen years.

Along the way, Super Fred became an icon of sportsmanship for a memorable act of compassion; bowled an over at Ricky Ponting, which will be talked about for years; overtook Ian Botham's Ashes record by hitting no less than nine sixes in a Test; won himself the freedom of his home town of Preston; earned himself an MBE; and gave the nation a chuckle over the breakfast table as they read newspaper reports of Freddie enjoying the mother of all Ashes-winning celebratory benders.

As if that was not enough, he ended the year staring stylishly out of a top-selling portrait calendar, was voted the ICC's joint Player Of The Year and the Professional Cricketers Association's Player Of The Year, and he was also the overwhelming winner of the BBC Sports Personality Of The Year trophy. By any standards, it was an extraordinary few months for an extraordinary cricketer – even his stubble was voted Beard Of The Year and *GQ* magazine named him as the 72nd most powerful man in Britain.

Long before the Australian touring party arrived in the spring of 2005, Ashes fever was gripping the country. The Test matches were all sold out well in advance and the good news from England's point of view was that Freddie's recuperation was going according to plan.

Physio Dave Roberts was anxious his charge should not try to do too much too soon and he paced Freddie's recovery accordingly. The signs were encouraging from the moment Freddie hit a comeback 100 in an early-season knock and, crucially, he was bowling again seemingly without discomfort after his operation.

In the One-Day Internationals, Freddie's England team-mates noticed he didn't quite seem to be himself, but it was understandable as he felt his way back to full match fitness. By the time the First Test at Lord's came around, however, he was champing at the bit.

Much of the hype leading up to the game centred around Freddie playing his first Test match against Australia after waiting seven years and forty-eight Test matches since making his international debut – an England record by some distance. The expectation was huge and Freddie was desperate not to disappoint.

But, as he later admitted, he was so wound up wanting to do well in his first confrontation with the Aussies at Test level that it had an adverse effect. Freddie put too much pressure on himself and he had a game largely to forget as Australia won the First Test convincingly by 239 runs.

His long-delayed first Test innings against the Aussies lasted just four balls when he was comprehensively bowled by McGrath for a duck by one which cut back and kept a little low. So much had been expected of him and he trudged back to the Lord's pavilion with the England scoreboard showing a dismal 21 for 5.

He fared little better in the second innings, caught behind

off Warne, and in the field he put down what for Freddie was a routine catch at slip. He did have the consolation, however, of twice in the match taking the prize wicket of the dangerous Adam Gilchrist.

Despite two defiant half-centuries from Test debutant Kevin Pietersen, England slumped to a crushing defeat, and McGrath rubbed it in by forecasting Australia would whitewash England five–nil. That was a prediction the Barmy Army would gleefully throw back at the great bowler on many occasions later in the summer.

Freddie's bitter disappointment at his own performance was enough for him to take himself off to Devon for a few days with Rachael and Holly to put it out of his mind. Later, he sought advice and help from sports psychologist Jamie Edwards and they spoke together about Freddie's mental approach at Lord's which clearly had not been right. 'I like to be relaxed when I play cricket, but at Lords I wasn't,' he explained. 'I was wound up, I was uptight, I wasn't me.'

He reported for duty at Edgbaston refocused and in a much more positive frame of mind. He determined he would play his natural game, enjoy himself and play to his natural strengths.

When Ricky Ponting won the toss for Australia, the England team and supporters could hardly believe it when he opted to field first on a batsman-friendly track, especially as Glenn McGrath had turned his ankle over in the warm-up and would take no part in the match.

England made Ponting pay by posting a first-day total of

407, which astonishingly included no less than fifty-four boundaries and ten sixes. Even numbers ten and eleven, Steve Harmison and Simon Jones, managed to clear the rope once each. England's score was their highest total on the opening day of a Test against Australia for sixty-seven years and their attacking intent set the tone for the rest of the series.

When it was Freddie's turn to bat, he was lucky to survive early on when he checked a drive midway through the stroke and succeeded in merely chipping the ball up in the air. Luckily for him, it just cleared the fielder at mid-off. After that let-off, Freddie was never so tentative again. He proceeded to play with customary freedom and to treat the crowd to the kind of innings they had come to expect from him.

He attacked the bowling with conviction and a relish which brought him five sixes and six fours. Three of Freddie's sixes came off Warne and two off Lee, including one thrilling hook off his eyebrows. By the time he was out for 68 made off 62 balls, the Australians had been left in no doubt that everything they had heard about Freddie's awesome hitting was true.

On day two, England's bowlers worked their way though the Australian batting line-up to dismiss them for 308, Freddie finishing off the innings with two successful LBW shouts in successive balls to finish with 3 for 52.

The lead of 99 was more than useful, but England were tottering at 72 for 5 in their second innings on the morning of day three when Freddie came out to bat at number seven, Hoggard having been promoted the night before to night watchman. That rapidly became 75 for 6 leaving Freddie the job of rescuing the innings – and the match – with just the tail to come.

There soon followed an anxious passage of play after Freddie suddenly recoiled in pain clutching his left shoulder while executing a powerful cut. It was several minutes before he could resume batting, having received treatment on the field from the England physio, and he was still in obvious pain. He was relieved to make it through the twenty minutes to lunch where he could receive further treatment.

Happily, Freddie emerged after the interval showing few signs of discomfort, but wickets continued to fall at the other end. At 131 for 9, England's lead was a precarious 230 when last man Simon Jones joined Freddie and it was the signal for him to launch an incredible assault on the bowling.

Kasprowicz, playing in place of the unfit McGrath, was the first to suffer as Freddie crashed him for 20 in one over including two sixes, the second of which brought up his 50.

The bowler was swiftly withdrawn to be replaced by Lee, but it didn't make any difference. Freddie proceeded to drill two more incredible sixes straight back over the bowler's head, one enormous blow depositing the ball on the roof of the pavilion where it was retrieved by Graham Gooch with the help of a TV cameraman. In all Freddie plundered 18 from the over despite Lee posting his nine fielders around the boundary.

It was a phenomenal display of hitting which regularly brought the crowd to their feet in raptures. With Jones,

Freddie added a priceless 51 runs for the last wicket and the incredible entertainment ended only when Freddie went for another big hit, missed and was bowled by Warne for 73. It was Warne's 599th Test wicket.

During his explosive innings, Freddie hit four more sixes to add to the five he hit in England's first innings. This total of nine in the match beat Ian Botham's Ashes record of six in a single Test.

Freddie walked off to a standing ovation the like of which an Edgbaston crowd has rarely been moved to deliver. The applause and cheers were deafening. Wishing to add his congratulations, Warne had to chase after Freddie on his way back to the pavilion to make himself heard above the din. Finally, he caught Freddie's attention, clapped his hands and said, 'Well batted, Freddie. Well played, mate.'

Freddie had changed the game in the most sensational manner. Batting last, Australia now had to chase a victory target of 282. Crucially, England's last wicket partnership had turned it from a very attainable target to one that would take some getting.

Australia's openers, Hayden and Langer, however, looked in no difficulty and they had put on 47 when Vaughan turned to Freddie to make the breakthrough. After the shoulder injury he had wrenched while batting, no one was quite sure how it would affect his bowling.

The crowd were, however, aware that Freddie was on a hat-trick, having taken two wickets with successive balls to end

Australia's first innings, and they roared his every step on his run-up to the wicket to deliver his first ball.

Langer safely negotiated it, but next delivery he pushed forward and the ball cannoned off his armguard on to his thigh and thence on to the stumps. Freddie had taken three wickets in four balls.

The crowd erupted, and the ground was still buzzing when Ricky Ponting took guard and prepared to face a fired-up Freddie who was bowling at over 90mph. What followed was sheer drama and made for a totally unforgettable over.

Freddie's first ball to Ponting was fired in at great pace, swung late and rapped him on the pads. A roared appeal went up but umpire Billy Bowden turned it down. Ponting tried to look composed and unruffled but inside he must have been mightily relieved.

Freddie's next ball was again of searing pace and Ponting played a thoroughly unconvincing half-push shot which saw the ball drop short of Giles at fourth slip.

Ponting was clearly unsettled, and the next ball was another fast inswinger which again crashed into his pads but outside the line of the off-stump. Another vociferous appeal once again left Billy Bowden unmoved.

The tension around the ground was electric as Freddie turned to run in and deliver the sixth ball of the over. The Australian captain managed to get his bat out of the way as it flashed through to Geraint Jones outside the off-stump. Believing it was the end of the over, a relieved Ponting was starting to move out of his crease to walk up the wicket to have a word with Hayden when he realised it had been a no-ball. He had one more ball to face – and it was his last.

Tearing in once more, Freddie produced a big outswinger on a perfect line and length, forcing Ponting to play at it and Edgbaston once more went wild as he got a nick through to keeper Jones. Ponting looked shattered as he departed while Freddie simply stood with back arched and arms outstretched as he was engulfed by his joyful teammates.

'What an over!' Richie Benaud declared to the millions of TV viewers.

'That over was probably the best I've ever bowled,' Freddie said afterwards. 'I was slightly lucky to get Langer, but then I sent down a few decent balls at Ponting. The ball was reverse-swinging, coming back into the right-hander, and I thought I'd just swap it around and see if it went away from him. It did, and it was great.'

Freddie's incredible dismantling of Ponting, one of modern cricket's greatest batsmen, was compared to the famous over bowled by Michael Holding to Geoff Boycott in Barbados in the 1980–81 series in the West Indies. Then, 'Whispering Death', as Holding was known for his wonderfully smooth run-up, beat Boycott all ends up five balls in a row before bowling him with his sixth.

In all, Freddie had taken 4 Australian wickets in 9 balls, and Michael Vaughan was not alone when he later said he felt that Freddie's over had been the turning point of the series.

England's bowlers continued to make inroads into the Australian batting and, when Harmison produced a clever slower ball to bowl Clarke in the last over of the day, it left Australia on 175 for 8 at the close and staring at defeat.

The following tension-filled day saw Australia starting off needing 107 to win with just the 2 wickets left. But one of those was Warne and he proceeded to give the wonderfully supportive Edgbaston crowd the jitters by mixing stout defence with lusty blows, which took Australia in sight of an improbable win.

Millions more were equally engrossed watching on television as the epic battle reached its final gripping stages. Again, it was Freddie who made the vital breakthrough when he forced Warne back in his crease and his foot slipped and dislodged the bails. Warne was out hit wicket for a fighting 42 leaving Australia with 62 still needed and Brett Lee going well.

Last man Kasprowicz more than held his end up, and gradually he and Lee whittled down the victory target.

Freddie was mixing up his deliveries and trying everything he knew to try to take the final wicket. But Lee, in particular, showed great courage standing up to the barrage, which included Freddie hitting him painfully on the hand.

The crowd grew progressively quieter as Australia inched towards the finishing line. They had arrived expecting England to wrap up a comfortable victory and now they were subdued and biting their nails at the prospect of defeat. But they were out of their seats when, with just 15 needed,

Kasprowicz sliced a Flintoff delivery in the air to third man where Simon Jones, normally the safest pair of hands in the field, threw himself forward and spilled the chance.

Soon there was just 4 needed. A single shot could now give Australia a remarkable victory, and Lee almost achieved it when he smacked a Harmison full toss towards the cover boundary. A couple of yards either side and it would have been all over but Simon Jones was on the rope to field the ball and restrict the batsman to a single.

That left Kasprowicz on strike, and 2 balls later Harmison induced the batsman to fend off a lifter down the leg side and straight into the gloves of wicketkeeper Jones.

England had won an absolute thriller by 2 runs, the narrowest margin in the 128-year history of the Ashes.

At the moment of victory, there was bedlam in the crowd and the England players converged upon each other, leaping and whooping with joy while Brett Lee sank to his knees in utter dejection. His brave innings of 43 not out had so nearly won the day. But now, head bowed in his moment of despair, he suddenly felt a comforting arm on his shoulder and a large hand clutching his in a handshake. It wasn't Kasprowicz commiserating with him – it was Freddie.

In England's moment of triumph, while his teammates were hugging each other, Freddie chose to seek out non-striker Lee and squatted down in front of him to console him and offer his own words of commiseration and admiration for Lee's courageous effort.

This supreme act of sportsmanship became the sporting image of the summer, and the photograph of this moment of human kindness and decency was reprinted time and again in newspapers and magazines. It said much about the spirit in which the series was played, and it said even more about Flintoff the man.

All morning in the heat of battle Freddie had been firing the ball down at Lee, hitting him on the elbow and on the hand, and the Aussie fast bowler had taken it all and fought on, only to see his efforts come to nothing. Now, with the game over, Freddie wanted to console his adversary and say as one cricketer to another, 'Well played.'

It had been a great team effort by England, but there was no doubting who was Man Of The Match. Freddie's two blistering half-centuries and his seven wickets, including that memorable over at Ponting, made him an automatic choice. Now it was one win each with three to play, and Freddie had really set the Ashes alight.

CHAPTER 16

A Ton Up In Notts

'I was experiencing emotions I've never felt before through cricket. I was a complete mess.'

ANDREW FLINTOFF ON THE THRILLING CLIMAX TO THE FOURTH TEST AT NOTTINGHAM

If Australia thought they had seen enough of Freddie at Edgbaston, they arrived at Old Trafford for the Third Test to find he was virtually omnipresent. Cardboard cutouts of Freddie – advertising a beer – were everywhere, and the real Freddie was extra keen to do well in front of his home crowd.

A masterful 166 by Michael Vaughan, after being bowled by a McGrath no-ball, put England in charge of the match on the first day which saw Warne take his 600th Test wicket.

By the time Freddie went out to bat, England already had a healthy score of 341 and it allowed him to play his strokes from the start in a breezy knock of 46 which ended when he was caught at long-off going for another big hit.

England continued to dominate the match and would surely have won if the weather had not intervened. In between the stoppages for rain, England worked their way into a powerful position whereby they could declare their second innings leaving Australia to make a mammoth 423 to win.

It was all set up for a fascinating finish and such was the clamour for bargain-priced last-day tickets that the gates were closed at 8.30am and many thousands were turned away. The lucky ones who got in were to witness another extraordinarily nerve-racking climax – and another manful effort from Freddie.

While Ricky Ponting stood firm, England took wickets at regular intervals and seemed on course for victory when Ponting was finally out for a gritty rearguard 156. Once again, Freddie was in the forefront of England's push for victory taking 4 for 71. The fall of Warne's wicket even prompted him to execute a mid-pitch back-flip by way of celebration.

Agonisingly for England, in mounting tension Australia managed to hang on for a draw with just one wicket remaining.

There was much debate in informed cricketing circles as to whether it was England or Australia who would have the momentum going into the Fourth Test at Trent Bridge.

Australia could feel that England had missed a golden opportunity to take a two–one lead in the series at Old Trafford. Not taking that chance was something they might live to bitterly regret. England, on the other hand, could point to the fact that they had outplayed Australia in that game and, but for rain, would almost certainly have emerged as winners.

Naturally, they were disappointed not to have taken that last Australian wicket, but they could take heart from the Australian team's reaction to escaping defeat. No one could remember seeing an Aussie side displaying such euphoria over managing to scrape a draw.

Of all the England's players, Freddie felt the exertions of the last day at Old Trafford the most. Michael Vaughan had called him up to bowl no less than 25 overs in the day, the highest number of overs he had ever sent down in a single day's play.

It was a Herculean effort, but it left him exhausted both mentally and physically. To clear his head and get right away from cricket, Freddie, Rachael and Holly took a short break in St Tropez. Thankfully for him, he went almost entirely unrecognised and therefore unpestered in the South of France resort and it proved to be a welcome and worthwhile few days away. He returned refreshed and yet again played a significant role in determining the outcome of the game.

Michael Vaughan started the day well for England by winning the toss and choosing to bat and, on a rain-affected first day, Freddie arrived at the crease with England 213 for 4.

As the ground filled up before the start of play on the second day, the crowd were eagerly anticipating the prospect of Freddie and Kevin Pietersen batting together. But it was not long before Pietersen was caught behind off Lee to make it 241 for 5.

England now needed Freddie to consolidate and push the

total up to more than just a respectable score and, not for the first time in Tests, he found the perfect partner in Geraint Jones. In company with the wicketkeeper, Freddie proceeded to bat Australia out of the match and score his first Test century against the Aussies in the process.

He may have played some brutal innings for England in the past few years, but this wasn't Freddie trying to belt the cover off the ball. This was Freddie at his masterful best – cool, deliberate, controlled and playing glorious, orthodox cricket shots.

To the fast bowlers, Freddie presented the full face of the bat, and against Shane Warne he carefully reined himself in unless the ball was there to be hit. Occasionally, it was, and he dropped to one knee to smite a leg stump Warne half-volley into the Fox Road stand over midwicket for six to bring up his half-century.

When Ponting called up twenty-two-year-old debutant Shaun Tait with the new ball, Freddie effortlessly leaned into some imperious drives which raced through the covers to the boundary. They were strokes of supreme power and timing.

Finally, after some nervous moments on 99, Freddie was able to nudge Warne on the leg side for a comfortable single to reach a magnificent century. Undetected by the spectators, but not by sharp-eyed television viewers, Freddie allowed himself a wink at Warne as he jogged past the bowler to complete the run.

The ground erupted when he reached three figures and,

as Freddie removed his helmet and raised his bat in acknowledgement, he reserved a lingering look of appreciation for Rachael sitting in the crowd with little Holly perched on her knee.

Freddie's superb knock ended soon afterwards when he was trapped LBW for 102 made off 132 balls with fourteen fours and a six. With Jones, he had put on 177 and his 100 went a long way to helping England eventually reach an impressive first innings total of 477, their highest in a Test at Trent Bridge for sixty-seven years.

It was a vital knock for his side but, on a personal level, Freddie's innings also marked the moment when his Test batting average climbed above his Test bowling average for the first time – the mark of a true all-rounder.

It was Freddie's fifth Test 100, his best, and hugely satisfying for the big man in that it came on the ground where he had made such an unremarkable Test debut seven years earlier.

When it was Australia's turn to bat, they quickly subsided to 99 for 5 by the close of play. The following morning Freddie got rid of danger man Adam Gilchrist for the fourth time in the series, thanks to a stupendous catch at slip by Strauss who threw himself full length to take the ball in his outstretched left hand.

Eventually, Australia were all out for 218 and found themselves in the unaccustomed position of having to follow on. But England's task of bowling them out a second time was made considerably harder when Simon Jones, who had taken 5 wickets in the first innings, left the field with an ankle injury after bowling just 4 overs.

It left England a bowler short, but patiently they worked their way through the Australian batsmen to leave themselves the seemingly simple victory target of 129.

When the openers Strauss and Trescothick put on 32 for the first wicket, England looked to be sailing along serenely. Then, enter Warne. With his first ball, he dismissed Trescothick, and in a flash he had also bamboozled Vaughan for a duck and had Strauss caught for 1.

At the other end, Lee was working up a furious pace and, when he coaxed Bell into an ill-judged hook which landed in the safe hands of Kasprowicz, Freddie found himself walking to the wicket with England reeling at 57 for 4 and Australia sensing they could pull off a most dramatic win.

In the next 10 overs, Pietersen and Freddie steadied the ship, each finding the boundary three times as they took the score to 103 before Pietersen flashed at Lee and was caught behind with England still 26 runs short.

Still there seemed no real sense of alarm. Freddie was looking solid, and surely he and Geraint Jones would see the job through. But with the score at 111, Lee, who was regularly bowling at 95mph, ripped a snorter through Freddie's defence to hit the top of his off-stump. Freddie was gone for 26, a modest score, but, in the context of the match situation, those runs were priceless.

The sight of England's champion trudging back to the pavilion after being bowled so comprehensively stunned the crowd who had been cheering every run.

Back in the pavilion, Freddie found himself unable to watch what was going on in the middle as Geraint Jones then proceeded to hole out at long off to leave England on 116 for 7. The tension was unbearable and Freddie took himself off to the showers leaving Simon Jones to bring him regular reports of England's progress. It was left to Giles and Hoggard to inch their way to the target with just Harmison and the injured Simon Jones to bat if need be.

After Hoggard surprisingly drove Lee through the off-side for four, Freddie felt able to emerge from the showers to watch Giles finally punch Warne through midwicket to bring England home by 3 wickets.

At the moment of victory, Freddie was out on the pavilion balcony, his face a remarkable picture of emotion. In sharp contrast to the cool expression he wore when raising his bat for his century, now he looked pumped up like no one had ever seen him before. Trent Bridge's Man Of The Match was wild-eyed, mouth open roaring defiance and relief, his right arm cocked as though he was about to deliver a Lennox Lewis-style upper cut. 'When Ashley scored the winning runs I was experiencing emotions I've never felt before through cricket. I was a complete mess,' he later admitted.

For the third Test in a row, it had been another nail-biting last day, an astonishing finish to a game that could have gone either way.

Freddie's extraordinary display of emotion was understandable. It would have been cruel on the England team to lose having dominated the entire match for all but the last session of play. It would have been especially hard on Freddie after his splendid century, his 3 wickets in the match and his vital steadying innings of 26 when Australia were pressing for a shock win at the death.

Amid the general euphoria, the stark fact was sinking in that England were now two–one up in the series with one to play. They would require just a draw at the Oval to win back the Ashes.

CHAPTER 17

Ashes Regained

'Behind these sunglasses there's a thousand stories'

ANDREW FLINTOFF TO DAVID GOWER AT THE TRAFALGAR SQUARE ASHES VICTORY PARADE

Throughout the series, England's team had virtually picked itself, notwithstanding continuous debate – among England fans at least – about the merits of persevering with Geraint Jones behind the stumps.

When Channel 4 commentator Mark Nicholas picked up on the subject and suggested some people felt Jones's glovework was not what it might be, Freddie shot back, 'Not in our dressing room, they don't.' It was a telling riposte from Freddie and an indication of the one-for-all team spirit in the England camp.

But it was the other Jones who was causing concern going into the Fifth Test. Despite desperate efforts to get Simon Jones fit for the Fifth Test at the Oval after his serious injury at Nottingham, he bowed to the inevitable which left the selectors with a real dilemma. Should they pick James Anderson to bowl in his place? Or opt for a more safety-first approach and choose Paul Collingwood, primarily a batsman who can bowl?

In the event, Collingwood got the nod with England's remaining pace attack of Freddie, Steve Harmison and Matthew Hoggard all vowing that, in Simon's absence, they would bear the additional load with spinner Giles to accommodate the extra batsman.

Once Vaughan had won the toss and chosen to take first use of the best batting track in the country, England's objective was clear: bat well, occupy the crease and post a big total that would effectively bat Australia out of the game.

The openers Trescothick and Strauss got England off to a near-perfect start with an array of fine strokes. In just 17 overs, they made 82 together, but Shane Warne then turned the game on its head by taking 4 wickets for 22 runs.

Suddenly, England were 131 for 4 and in danger when Freddie walked out to join Strauss who had just reached his 50. Together, they stopped the rot and, urged on by an appreciative crowd basking in bright sunshine, they shared a crucial partnership of 143 before Freddie was caught behind.

He had hauled England out of trouble with another mature innings of 72, which included a big six off Warne which sailed into the new £25 million OCS Stand at the Vauxhall End of the ground. Freddie departed with England on 274 for 5, a healthy enough score but well short of the commanding total England were aiming for. It was left to Strauss, making his second century of the series, and a valuable 32 from Giles to haul England up to a respectable but far from impregnable total of 373.

When Australia began their reply, Hayden and Langer at last began to look for the first time in the series the formidable opening pair their records suggested. But, when they had put on 112 together, the umpires offered them the chance to go off because of bad light. To the amazement of the England team and their supporters, the batsmen accepted and walked off.

It was a baffling decision considering the onus was on Australia to win the match to retain the Ashes. It didn't make sense – there was no way the Aussies were going to forge a winning position with the players off the field. Their argument was that it was vitally important not to lose wickets, but the England players were quite happy to let time slip away.

Over the next two days, there was the bizarre situation of a packed partisan Oval crowd, who had paid good money for their tickets, now praying for rain and no play at all. The England fans would be content with a draw, however it was achieved.

In between the showers and the bad light, Australia pressed on with Hayden and Langer both hitting centuries, and the third day ended with the Aussies just 96 runs behind

England's total with 8 wickets in hand. There was no doubt that they were in a strong position, but in the last session Freddie struck an important blow by having Ponting caught off a ball of extra bounce.

The following morning, the newspapers were full of bravado emanating from the Australian camp. Their plan, they said, was to bat on well past England's total and get a lead of perhaps 150 or 200 in order to put the pressure back on the home side to save the game. They reckoned they would have a great chance of victory on the final day with England having to face Warne on a wearing fifth-day pitch.

But Freddie had other ideas. He hadn't played out of his skin all series just to be thwarted at the last. He arrived at the Oval on day four determined to carry on his good work from the night before when he had nipped out Australia's skipper. He exhorted the rest of the team to give their all and proceeded to give a remarkable demonstration of practising what he preached.

Bowling unchanged from the start of play to just before tea, he produced a marathon spell of aggressive fast bowling which completely changed the course of the match. For sheer heart, skill, courage, perseverance, and sustained energy, it was one of the most remarkable and consistently hostile spells ever witnessed at the Oval.

First, he induced Martyn to lob a catch to midwicket then trapped Hayden LBW. Next over, Katich went the same way as Hayden. Finally, he claimed Warne for a duck and, with

Hoggard taking wickets at the other end, Australia lost their last seven batsmen for 44 runs.

Instead of staring at a large first-innings deficit, England had a lead of 6 runs and Freddie finished with the exceptional figures of 34 overs, 10 maidens and 5 wickets for 78 runs. In all, counting his spell on the Saturday evening, England's Colossus had bowled 18 overs unchanged. He had totally altered the course of the game with the bat and now he had done it again with the ball.

By the close, England had increased that lead to 40 for the loss of 1 wicket. The destiny of the Ashes would be decided on the final day. And, as it turned out, not until the final session of the series.

It would have set the seal on Freddie's summer of heroics if he had made a major contribution on the last day of the Fifth Test. But it was not be. Instead, it was Kevin Pietersen who won the day with a thrilling innings of 158, including seven sixes, after England had wobbled alarmingly in the middle of their innings.

During another day's cricket of almost unbearable tension, it became clear that the game was far from safe when Vaughan and Bell departed in quick succession, followed soon afterwards by Freddie who carved a boundary before hitting a return catch back to Warne. If the innings had quickly crumbled, Australia would have had enough overs in which to launch a victory assault with the bat.

But Pietersen boldly took the attack to the Aussies, ably

supported first by a stubbornly defensive Collingwood and then by Giles, who hit his highest Test score of 59, until it became apparent that, whatever happened, Australia would not have enough time to win the game. The match was drawn and England had won the Ashes.

For Freddie and the rest of the England team, the lap of honour around the Oval in front of a delirious crowd is a moment they will cherish all their lives.

Freddie was duly nominated England's Man Of The Series by Aussie coach John Buchanan after scoring more than 400 runs at an average of over 40 and taking 24 wickets. He was also the recipient of the inaugural Compton-Miller medal for the Man Of The Series chosen from both sides.

One worthy statistic which escaped much attention was that Freddie had bowled 194 overs in the series, more than any other England bowler by some distance – and 70 more than Hoggard. It showed how much Vaughan had relied upon his all-rounder.

Such deeds with both bat and ball prompted inevitable comparisons with Ian Botham's Ashes series in 1981. Some experts considered Freddie's was the better achievement given the comparative strengths of the Australian teams.

Sir Gary Sobers, in London promoting the 2007 World Cup in the West Indies, had no doubts. The man regarded as the greatest all-rounder ever was quoted as saying, 'Flintoff builds his innings more so than Ian. That's the reason I feel Flintoff is a better all-rounder. Ian would go in and play a lot of shots and if he got out people would say that's the way he plays. In a difficult situation, as you saw in the Ashes, Flintoff went in and he got himself on top and then he started to explode.'

Looking back over the series, Shane Warne used his column in *The Times* to say, 'Andrew Flintoff was the big star. He deserves every award he has picked up. He would be an asset to any side in the world, in the dressing room and on the field. We have become good mates, although nobody could dislike Freddie. He's one of the nice guys and he drags the party along. He even opens the bottles of beer for you with his teeth.'

Glenn McGrath described Freddie as currently the best cricketer in the world, and Australia's vice-captain Adam Gilchrist rated Freddie on a par with Warne. 'Those are the two most valuable guys you would want in your team,' he said.

Former Australian skipper Richie Benaud went so far as to hail Freddie as a possible England captain in years to come. 'He lifted himself on several occasions during the series. I think Andrew Flintoff is a future England captain, at least of the One-Day International side,' Benaud told BBC World Service. 'It depends how Michael Vaughan goes in the One-Day Internationals, but certainly I would be looking at him as vice-captain in the next team to go away to give him a bit of experience; he is a thinker.'

If Freddie was undoubtedly the star of the series, there was no question that he was also the star of the victory celebrations. Just as he'd done on the field in his lion-hearted bowling spell, now he showed incredible stamina to keep celebrating and make merry through the evening, right through the night and throughout the following day's victory parade as well until he eventually fell asleep on the team coach.

Every celebratory sip was gleefully chronicled in the newspapers: first, there was post-match victory champagne, then a few beers with Steve Harmison. Both family men, they chose not to go out on the town clubbing with other teammates but to spend the night in the hotel bar where, asked about his new celebrity status, Freddie declared, 'I'm ugly, I'm overweight, but I'm happy. I'd never make a decent celebrity.'

He was, however, genuinely pleased at the news that the Mayor of Preston had announced that Freddie was to be given the freedom of his home town. 'It means I can drive a flock of sheep through the town centre, drink for free in no less than 64 pubs and get a lift home with the police when I become inebriated,' he said. 'What more could you want?'

At 6.30am, he was reported to have had a gin and tonic and a vodka and cranberry juice just to freshen up before attending the champagne breakfast at the hotel at 8.30am where former England captain Mike Gatting asked him if he'd had anything to eat. 'Yes,' replied Freddie. 'A cigar.'

Television cameras captured Freddie looking worse for wear and stepping unsteadily out of the hotel near Tower Bridge as the team headed off to board the open-top bus which would take them on a victory parade through the streets of London.

There was more champagne swigged straight from the

bottle as the bus slowly made its way through cheering crowds towards Trafalgar Square where thousands of people had gathered to greet the team. Also waiting for Freddie, microphone at the ready, was former England captain David Gower wanting a chat with cricket's man of the hour.

It may not have been the most opportune moment to capture Freddie for a few words but he was the one the crowd wanted to hear from. 'To be honest with you, David, I'm struggling,' Freddie managed to say. 'I've not been to bed yet, and the eyes behind these glasses tell a thousand stories. The emotional journey we have been through – it's just fantastic and we are enjoying it.'

Later he said, 'I think I'm still dreaming – winning the Ashes is something I've thought about since I was a kid. I'm sure it will take a while to realise the enormity of what's happened. For goodness' sake, we've won the Ashes. It's massive. When we were on top of that bus, driving through the streets of London, it was a brilliant feeling. I was a bit worried three people would turn up waving a single flag.

'I don't know if this will change my life – you'll probably have to ask me that in a week or so. But, no matter what happens, I'm not going to stop doing the things I do.'

Like the rest of the players, Freddie was utterly overwhelmed by the reception given to the team and the sheer size of the crowd who thronged Trafalgar Square to cheer their heroes.

Next, it was on to Downing Street for a 1.30pm welcome

from the Prime Minister and more beer hastily produced after an aide's initial offer of sparkling water and soft drinks was quickly rejected.

Then it was on to Lord's at 3pm and more champagne, followed at 6pm by toasting of the sponsor, Vodafone, with yet more champagne.

Finally, there was the victory dinner at 8pm, which prompted captain Michael Vaughan to say, 'My next biggest challenge is to survive another night with Freddie.'

Even someone with Freddie's constitution has to sleep sometime, and he finally nodded off in the team coach back to the hotel. He emerged with a dark moustache, goatee beard and specs inked on to his face and the word 'Twat' written across his forehead, courtesy of Steve Harmison. Freddie had no idea he was displaying Harmison's artful artwork as he staggered off the bus.

It says much for the general affection for Freddie that, at a time when there was much public debate about how the government should tackle binge drinking, very few begrudged him his very public 32-hour-long celebration.

Before the series started, Freddie had said that, if England won back the Ashes, nothing would ever be the same again for the players involved. He was absolutely right, but he wasn't quite prepared for the Freddie fever which swept the country.

Quite apart from the requests for autographs and the back-slapping that he encountered everywhere he went for months after the Ashes triumph, Freddie was voted Beard Of The

Year, signed up to pose for a calendar and found himself splashed across the front cover of *Hello!*, a magazine usually reserved for its pictures and interviews with royalty, supermodels and showbusiness stars. Inside, he was pictured looking slightly uncomfortable snuggled up with Rachael on a beanbag. There was even talk of his making a CD of his favourite songs and there was an approach from Donatella Versace to kit him out in Versace clothes.

There were predictions that Freddie's annual earnings could top £3 million if he cared to take up offers to add to the advertising and promotional deals he already had with Red Bull, Thwaites, Volkswagen, the *Sun*, Barclays and Woodworm. PR guru Max Clifford said, 'Flintoff is good-looking, the man of the series and has shown great spirit, like when he commiserated with Australia after the second game. He's the superstar and the sky's the limit for him. He could easily earn £3 million in the next twelve months through sponsorship deals.'

That, of course, was something largely for his management team to consider, not least because Freddie had plenty else to occupy his mind.

To their delight, Rachael found she was expecting their second child in the spring and the couple decided to find a new home for their growing family. By the autumn, they had moved into a magnificent new house – soon nicknamed Fredingham Palace by the tabloids – in a smart area of Cheshire.

The furniture had barely arrived before Freddie had to head

off down under with Steve Harmison in early October to play for the Rest Of The World against Australia. The Australians would be getting their first real look at the Pom who, more than any other, had helped wrest away the Ashes. Until then, Freddie had made just one appearance in an international in Australia.

Freddie's compassionate gesture in consoling Brett Lee at the end of the Edgbaston Test had gone down exceptionally well with the Australian public and ensured he was given a warm welcome. Freddie and Lee had exchanged signed blown-up copies of the photograph showing his moment of supreme sportsmanship, and on his travels Lee had not been backward in giving Australians his own personal assessment of Freddie: 'much better than awesome'.

On the eve of the ICC Super Series in Melbourne, Lee said, 'It will go down as one of the great moments in sportsmanship. He could have hugged his mates and celebrated but he chose to put his arm around me.

'They will take to him here because of the way he plays. When I walked around Melbourne yesterday, people were approaching me to ask about the games and then whether Freddie is as nice as he is on television. Kids are celebrating like Freddie with both hands in the air and their backs arched, and they've been getting his haircut.'

Fittingly, while he was in Australia, Freddie was named joint Player Of The Year with Jacques Kallis at a special ICC awards ceremony held at the Four Seasons Hotel in Sydney.

Both players finished level on eighty-six votes from the fifty-member voting Academy, the first tie in the short history of the ICC Awards.

ICC President Ehsan Mani commented, 'These two players made outstanding all-round contributions to the fortunes of their sides so it is wholly appropriate they should both receive the Sir Garfield Sobers Trophy, named after the greatest all-rounder of all time.

'The fact that they finished level, both polling more than twice as many votes as the player in third place, reflects their massive contributions to international cricket during the voting period.

'Andrew Flintoff consistently demonstrated his all-round excellence and his ability to turn a game with both bat and ball and marked him out as a real crowd-pleaser.

'Not content to contribute with bat and ball, both players also remained in the thick of the action in the field and proved outstanding catchers, especially in the slip cordon.

'The fact this award was voted for by the players' peers and colleagues is an illustration of the high regard in which they are held within the cricket community, and Jacques and Andrew are worthy recipients of this award.'

During the voting period of 1 August 2004 to 31 July 2005, Freddie played ten Tests and sixteen One-Day Internationals. In Tests, he scored 366 runs at an average of 30.50, including four scores of 50 or more, captured 44 wickets at an average of 24.68 and took 6 catches. Freddie took a wicket every 45.43 balls, a mark bettered by only four bowlers – Andre Nel, Mattiah Muralitharan, Glenn McGrath and Matthew Hoggard, all of them specialists rather than an all-rounder like Freddie.

He also scored 464 runs in One-Day Internationals at an average of 38.66 including one century and two other scores of 50 or more, and those runs were made at a strike-rate of 92.98. With the ball, he took 25 wickets with an economy rate of just 4.32 runs per over.

Australian cricket fans were given a glimpse of why Freddie was regarded as the world's premier all-rounder when he performed consistently well for the Rest Of The World in the One-Day Internationals.

In the Test at Sydney, he was even more impressive, taking 4 wickets for 59 in Australia's first innings, and another 3 for 48 in the second innings – Shane Watson becoming his 150th Test victim. He also scored 35 in the World XI's first innings.

In general, the cream of the world's cricketers performed well below par, losing all the One-Day Internationals and the Test to an Australian side desperate to get back to winning ways after the loss of the Ashes. But Freddie, initially flattered to be included in such exalted company, showed himself more than worthy of his place among them as the top all-rounder.

He left Australia hoping he could maintain his form for England in the upcoming tour of Pakistan, never the easiest of tours especially for fast bowlers on tracks more suited to spinners.

But, typically, Freddie put in another lion-hearted effort in the First Test to claim his best match haul of 8 wickets for 156 and also weighed in with an innings of 45.

Back in England, Freddie was becoming a shoe-in to win the BBC Sports Personality Of The Year award, but there was much speculation as to how he would be presented with the trophy. The BBC were keen to make it a live presentation, but that would mean Freddie staying up until the small hours because of the time difference with Pakistan. To complicate matters still further, England were scheduled to play a One-Day International against Pakistan the following day.

Television, as is customary these days, dictated matters and Freddie stayed up until 3am to receive his award. Fittingly, it was his boyhood idol, and now a good friend, Ian Botham, the last cricketer to win the award, who presented him with the trophy.

Arguments raged as to the wisdom of depriving England's pivotal talisman from his shuteye when the ceremony could so easily have been pre-recorded without serious detriment to the BBC's programme. Would Freddie have been allowed to stay up into the small hours if England were playing Australia the next day? It's doubtful. Hours later, the BBC's newly crowned sleep-deprived sporting hero was out for a duck, a limp pull ending in a catch at midwicket.

After all the euphoria surrounding the regaining of the Ashes, England came down with a bump and lost the Test series against Pakistan, although Freddie performed consistently. It was a disappointing end to an incredible year for England's cricketers.

Andrew Flintoff had collected just about every award going in 2005, and the new year started with yet another. It was announced that, along with his teammates, he had been awarded the MBE in the New Year's Honours list for bringing home the Ashes. Captain Michael Vaughan and coach Duncan Fletcher each received an OBE.

In its own way, 2006 was shaping up to be an even busier year for Freddie. Quite apart from tours to India and to Australia to defend the Ashes, there were two home Test series to be played in the summer, and it was also Freddie's benefit year, which would require his attendance at a wide range of functions. Generously, he had decided that a big chunk of his benefit earnings would go to charity including Ian Botham's leukaemia fund.

'Winning the Ashes has helped raise the profile of both cricket and the players, so hopefully that will help us raise more money for Leukaemia Research,' said Freddie. 'Ian has already raised over £6 million for the charity and hopefully we can play our part and give it a big boost this year.'

With Freddie also due to become a father for the second time, he made it plain that he planned to fly back in the middle of the India tour to be with Rachael at the birth. These days, England's cricketers have such permission written into their contracts and there was no way Freddie intended to miss out on the arrival of his child.

Rachael was due to give birth on 20 March, in the middle of the Third and final Test against India in Mumbai, and Freddie was determined to do everything he could to be with his wife. He told BBC Radio Five Live, 'I'd love to be there and I hope I will be. I'm just going to have to play it by ear a little bit. You can have plans and never quite know what's going to happen. But, if it's mid-Test, there's not a lot I can do.

'Andrew Strauss did it before Christmas in Pakistan and he had his critics, but it's something you desperately want to be at home for.'

Early in the New Year, he had an appointment to keep at Preston Town Hall to officially receive the freedom of Preston. Councillors had voted unanimously in favour of making Freddie an honorary Freeman of the city 'for his services and accomplishments' in cricket.

Only twenty-two people were given the honour in the last century, including footballer Sir Tom Finney in 1979 and Wallace and Gromit animator Nick Park in 1997.

In announcing the honour, Mayor Bikhu Patel said Flintoff was an excellent ambassador and role model and added, 'Andrew Flintoff may be an international cricket superstar these days, but he is Preston born and bred, and has always remained proud of his roots.

'He's a great role model and epitomises everything we want to portray Preston as – young, vibrant, enthusiastic and going places.

'He's been amazing in the Ashes and it seems only fitting

that his efforts should be recognised in this way, by joining the likes of Sir Tom Finney in becoming a Freeman of the city.'

Freddie was duly honoured on 21 January 2006 at the town hall, where he was robed and received a scroll at a special council chamber ceremony.

Hundreds of people turned out to watch the event and the route from the Guild Hall was lined with pupils from Freddie's former schools – City of Preston High School and Greenlands Primary – and youngsters from Harris Park and St Anne's, the cricket clubs where he first wielded a willow to such devastating effect.

Freddie was visibly moved by the reception he received. 'Since last summer, there have been a lot of accolades for me and the team, but this is right up there with the best of them, if not the best,' he told the assembled crowd. 'Being a Preston lad, having all this to go with it, all these people out here in the bitter cold, thank you very much.'

Looking on proudly were Freddie's parents and grandparents and the legendary Sir Tom Finney himself. Modest as ever, Freddie said, 'To be honoured by your home city and be on an elite list of people including Sir Tom Finney is something I never thought would happen when I was growing up here.

'Both my dad and my grandfather are always talking about Tom Finney and what a great sportsman he was and it's the same for everybody else in this city. So it makes me very proud to be on the list with him.'

Freddie conducted himself admirably throughout the ceremony, and he was on best behaviour again when he and Rachael went to Buckingham Palace in February to receive his MBE from the Queen.

He had been aware that his life, and the lives of all the players, would change immeasurably if England won the Ashes, but he can hardly have been prepared for the universal adulation that has come his way.

Astutely guided by Chubby Chandler and Neil Fairbrother at International Sports Management, Freddie is now one of the hottest commodities in the game. At a time when many were starting to chase Freddie's signature, The Woodworm Cricket Company made a swift move to sign him up in January 2003 after the company's launch of a complete range of cricket equipment in May 2002. 'Freddie is the perfect embodiment of the Woodworm brand,' said Woodworm's founder and managing director Joe Sillett when he announced he had secured Freddie's endorsement. 'He's ebullient, competitive and has a big future.' It was a timely signing, because Freddie has wielded Woodworm's patented Wand cricket bat to telling effect ever since.

After all the trials and tribulations of his early international career, Freddie has spectacularly turned his life around – which is a lesson in itself to youngsters everywhere and adds to his current standing within the game of cricket. He is hugely popular among his England colleagues who do not resent the glory that comes his way because he does not seek it or claim it. He plays for the team and not for his average. He doesn't set himself targets, personal landmarks are disregarded, and he shows rare understanding when a fielder puts down a catch off his bowling. He fields at slip, he stresses, so he knows that it isn't easy when the ball is flying off the edge.

When assessing Flintoff the superstar, one sports columnist wrote, 'It helps that he is a manifestly decent man.'

He is uncomplicated, affable, always ready to oblige a young fan with an autograph, and off the field likes to enjoy life without a hint of drawing attention to himself. He retains good friendships with mates whom he has known since before he was a sporting hero and who are nothing to do with cricket. On the field, his best friend is Steve Harmison. The big Durham fast bowler has never forgotten Freddie's support when he helped him through a terrible bout of homesickness while playing under Freddie's captaincy on an England A tour of Pakistan.

Stories of Freddie's decency abound. One oft-told example of his generosity involves a man in his sixties who is regularly to be found outside Old Trafford. The fellow likes to chat – not always coherently – to the players as they go through the gates. Freddie is prepared to lend an ear to what the fellow has to say without patronising him; he once gave him his England tie and has even put the man up in the hotel within the ground on a couple of occasions.

When asked recently how he would like to be remembered,

Freddie could have said many things – his 167 blitz at Edgbaston against the West Indies, 38 in an over off Alex Tudor, bowling Brian Lara for a duck, his Ashes triumphs and so on.

But it was none of those. No, Freddie knew how he would like to be remembered: 'As a good bloke.' His act of spontaneous sportsmanship towards Brett Lee will certainly enhance that image.

This exemplary moment inevitably came up for discussion when Freddie launched his testimonial with a sell-out banquet for 850 at St James' Park, Newcastle. The highlight of the evening was a Q and A session with compere Gabby Yorath asking questions of a panel consisting of Freddie himself, Steve Harmison and England and Newcastle striker Alan Shearer.

'Bearing in mind Andrew's outstanding display of sportsmanship towards Brett Lee, does the panel believe there is enough sportsmanship in sport?' asked Gabby.

The words were barely out of her mouth before Harmison picked up the baton. 'Can I stop that one?' said Freddie's great friend. 'Ten balls before the end of the game he hit Lee on the head twice, and on the arm and on the glove when he dropped his bat. So I'm not sure I'd call it sportsmanship.'

This verbal bouncer from Harmy might have floored some, but not Freddie. He summarily dispatched it in typically majestic Flintoff fashion and brought the entire place to their feet cheering his reply.

'Well,' said Freddie, a smile playing on his lips, 'I must

admit when I put my arm around him, the exact words I used were: "It's one–one, you Aussie bastard!"'

CHAPTER 18

Captain Fantastic

"This has been England's triumph, but especially it has been Flintoff's triumph. You worry about how long it will be before they wear him out, but the more they throw at him, the greater his response. He is a remarkable man."

SIMON BARNES OF THE TIMES AFTER ENGLAND'S THIRD TEST WIN OVER INDIA.

On 1 March, 2006, Freddie achieved a long-cherished ambition when he skippered England for the very first time in a Test Match, against India in Nagpur.

He was a very proud man, and recognized what a huge honour it was to be asked to lead the side in the first match of the Three Test series. But, as he readily admitted, the captaincy was something he wished he had inherited in very different circumstances.

Quite unexpectedly Freddie found himself appointed to the most prestigious job in the game after Michael Vaughan was forced to return home from the tour of India with the recurrence of a knee problem and vice-captain Marcus Trescothick soon followed for personal reasons.

With the Ashes-winning team further shorn of Ashley Giles

and Simon Jones due to injury, England were facing a major crisis and it was felt that Freddie was the man to face up and lead them out of it.

Freddie therefore became the first fully fledged, genuine all-rounder to captain England since Chris Cowdrey, who skippered the side in just one Test against West Indies in 1988.

Players both past and present were quick to back the decision taken by chairman of selectors David Graveney and coach Duncan Fletcher. 'Flintoff is an excellent choice to lead England,' said Nasser Hussain. 'He has a good cricket brain and this move will do him a lot of good.

'It will be a difficult task for him being an all-rounder,' Fletcher admitted. 'He hasn't captained for some time but we just believe he is the best man for the job, and the most important part of it is he is very keen. We believe he has the potential to lead the side efficiently, and what it might do is inspire him even more as a bowler and batter.'

In answering the call to the captaincy, Freddie immediately cancelled his plans to miss a Test to return home to be with Rachael for the birth of their second child.

'I've spoken with Rachael a couple of times over the last 48 hours and she's been very supportive,' he explained. 'I'm going to stay on, and then there's a window between the Tests and the one-dayers to get home and see the baby. It's a decision we've made together.

'The situation dictates what I'm doing. It is a sacrifice I

have had to make, but I feel I am very much making the right decision,' Freddie told the BBC.

'It is a hard decision, but Rachael is very supportive of it. She is very proud I have been made captain.

'Unfortunately I'm probably not going to get home until after the third Test match when the baby will be born. But looking at it realistically as well, the chances of Rachael going into labour and me flying home and getting it all on time were probably slim anyway.'

When news of Freddie's appointment as captain was made official, he received dozens of messages of congratulation from every corner of the cricketing world.

Ever since he first picked up a cricket bat he had dreamed of one day captaining England. Now his dream had come true and he was looking forward to it. 'I'm fully in control of my destiny now,' he said with a smile.

Because of injuries to senior players, the team Freddie led into the First Test was the youngest England had fielded for 40 years and included no less than three debutants in Alastair Cook, Ian Blackwell and Monty Panesar.

The first thing Freddie did right was to win the toss, and then he steadied England's ship in the first innings with a knock of 43 just when it looked as though England were throwing away the advantage of batting first.

In the on-field huddles before start of play, Freddie exhorted his young troops to make sure that they had given their all when they left the field at the end of every session of play.

Both Matthew Hoggard and Steve Harmison described Freddie's battle cries as inspirational and, given the disrupted pre-Test preparations, the team responded magnificently to emerge with a highly creditable draw having had the better of four-and-a-half of the five days.

Freddie admitted afterwards that he had enjoyed the experience of captaining the side. 'I didn't go in with any trepidation,' he said. 'I didn't feel at any point that it was too much for me or that I felt too tired. I'm very passionate about playing for England,' he stressed, 'and I was very proud to lead the side out.'

On the eve of the Second Test, Freddie was thrilled to receive the news that Rachael had given birth to a son, whom they named Corey. The baby boy weighed in at 6lb 14oz at Wythenshawe Hospital, near Manchester, having arrived ten days early.

For the new England cricket captain, it was the perfect end to what had been a very special week. And, as if by way of celebration, a few days later Freddie smote himself into the record books by hitting India's 17- year-old debutant spinner Chawla for two successive sixes, thereby going one better than Ian Botham's England record of 67 sixes in Test cricket. But Freddie's immense contribution of 70 and 51 with the bat, and four wickets with the ball, was not enough to prevent India winning the Second Test by nine wickets.

Freddie emerged from the Second Test defeat far from disheartened and believing England could win the final Test in Mumbai. He was firmly of the opinion that England did not deserve to lose the series and a victory would give them a creditable drawn series.

He might have thought his luck had temporarily deserted him when he lost the toss in Mumbai – the first time he had called incorrectly as England captain. But, to almost everyone's astonishment, India's captain Rahul Dravid chose to field first.

Dravid's inexplicable decision effectively handed England control of the match, largely thanks to a fine century from Strauss and 88 from debutant Owais Shah. Freddie himself hit 50 to take the England total to 400, and India were very much on the back foot when they conceded a first innings lead of 121.

Again leading by example, Freddie patiently worked his way to 50 in England's second innings to help set up a push for victory on the last day. It was Freddie's fourth consecutive half-century for England and by far the slowest of his Test career. He received some criticism for not trying to step up the run rate, but his tactics were fully vindicated on a sensational final day.

Needing 313 to win, India collapsed in dramatic fashion, losing seven wickets for 25 runs to be all out for 100. England had pulled off a remarkable victory by 212 runs.

India were still very much in the game at lunch with any

result still possible. But immediately after lunch Freddie induced Dravid – known as The Wall for his seemingly obdurate batting – into getting an edge into the gloves of Geraint Jones. When Udal then removed Tendulkar, England surged to victory.

For his two half centuries, his four wickets and his astute captaincy leading from the front, Freddie was named Man Of The Match. He was also named Man Of The Series for his tally of 272 runs and 13 wickets.

'To come to India and draw the series 1-1 against such a formidable side was a great effort from our lads,' said a delighted Freddie.

England coach Duncan Fletcher compared the achievement as on a par with winning the Ashes. And he said of Freddie: 'He did an outstanding job as captain.'

And once again, England's supporters, who numbered some 2,000 in Mumbai, were chanting in some corner of a foreign field a familiar refrain: 'Super Fred.'

As Freddie prepared to fly home to see his new-born son for the first time, he might have reflected just how much his fortunes had changed since he was last in India as an England cricketer. Then, he had been reduced to tears of frustration at his inability to cope with the Indian spinners; now, he was Man Of The Series, and captain of an England team that he had inspired to a famous win. Fittingly, Freddie arrived home to learn *Wisden* had named him The Leading Cricketer In The World.

The Rise and Rise of All-rounder Andrew Flintoff

6 December 1977 – Andrew Flintoff born in Preston.

1984 – Aged six, plays first game for Dutton Forshaw Under-Thirteens when they were one player short. Plays in a Manchester United tracksuit.

1987 season – Aged nine, plays for Lancashire Under-Elevens and hits first six.

1989 season – Joins St Anne's Cricket Club as a twelve-year-old junior player.

1990 – Hits 234, not out, in 20-overs game for St Anne's Under-Fifteens against Fordham Broughton.

1991 – Makes debut for England Under-Fifteens against Wales Under-Fifteens. First representation for his country.

1993 – Aged fifteen, makes his Second XI debut for Lancashire at Old Trafford again Glamorgan, scoring 26 and 13. Goes on England Schools' Under-Fifteens tour to South Africa.

SUMMER 1994 –Aged sixteen, wins a three-year contract with Lancashire County Cricket Club. Goes on 1994–5 England Under-Nineteens tour to West Indies.

24 AUGUST 1995 – Aged seventeen, makes First-Class county debut against Hampshire at Portsmouth. Makes 7 and 0, batting at number five. Bowls 4 overs for 15 runs in Hampshire's first innings and 7 overs for 24 in the second. Wicketless in both innings, but Lancashire won by 5 wickets.

1995 – Goes on 1995–6 England Under-Nineteens tour to Zimbabwe.

DECEMBER 1996 – Captains England Under-Nineteens on their 1996–7 tour of Pakistan and leads them to a one–nil series win in three Unofficial Tests. Makes 52 in first innings of First Unofficial Test at Faisalabad. England Under-Nineteens' second top scorer, with 200 runs.

24 JULY 1997 – Makes maiden County Championship century against Hampshire at Southampton. Hits one six and twenty-two fours in an innings of 117. *Wisden* described the knock as 'an innings of considerable maturity'.

1997 – Captains England Under-Nineteens against Zimbabwe. Goes on 1997–8 England A tour to Kenya and Sri Lanka.

JUNE 1998 – Awarded county cap. Hits 34 in an over by England pace bowler Alex Tudor in a County Championship match against Surrey at Old Trafford. Flintoff hit 6–4–4–4–4–6–6–0 in an over that included 2 no-balls. All the runs were scored on the leg side, and Flintoff missed the last ball and thus the chance to pass the record of 36 runs scored in an over held by Gary Sobers and Ravi Shastri. Flintoff was out for 61, made off 24 balls.

23 JULY 1998 – Makes England Test debut at Trent Bridge, Nottingham, against South Africa. Aged twenty years and 229 days, he becomes the youngest Lancashire cricketer to play for England. Takes his first Test wicket, having Jacques Kallis caught behind by Alec Stewart. Scores 17 in his first Test innings and gets out while trying to hit Kallis for six.

AUGUST 1998 – Bags a pair (a duck in both innings) in Fifth Test against South Africa at Headingley, Leeds, but takes vital catch to dismiss danger man Jonty Rhodes as England win by 23 runs, thus winning their first five-Test series for twelve years.

SEPTEMBER 1998 – Freddie's first One-Day Lord's final, during which Lancashire overwhelm Derbyshire by 9 wickets to win NatWest trophy.

1998 – Named fiftieth Cricket Writers' Club Young Player of the Year. Also named Professional Cricketers' Association's Young Player of the Year, but not selected for tour of Australia. Finishes third in Lancashire's County Championship batting averages, at 42.11, with a highest score of 160. Goes on 1998–9 England A tour to Zimbabwe and South Africa.

25 APRIL 1999 – At Chelmsford, blitzes 143 in 66 balls against Essex in CGU National League match, an amazing innings including nine sixes and fifteen fours totalling 114 in boundaries alone.

MAY 1999 – Picked for World Cup in England but plays little part. Goes on England's 1999–2000 tour of South Africa and Zimbabwe.

JANUARY 2000 – Breaks a toe during fourth over of the Fourth Test against South Africa and disappears from the England tour.

SEASON 2000 – Selected for home Zimbabwe series and for First Test against West Indies, but dropped after England's innings defeat. Recalled for NatWest One-Day series and wins Man Of The Match award after hitting 42, not out, off 45 balls against Zimbabwe. After controversy over his weight, greets award with comment, 'Not bad for a fat lad.'

26 JULY 2000 – Hits a match-winning 135, not out, for Lancashire against Surrey at the Oval in quarter-final of NatWest trophy. Former England captain David Gower says, 'We've just watched one of the most awesome innings we're ever going to see on a cricket field.' Flintoff's innings includes four sixes and nineteen fours.

24 OCTOBER 2000 – Chosen for tour of Pakistan. Hits 84 off 60 balls in England's successful 304-run chase in first One-Day International. This Man Of The Match Award-winning innings comes five days after he is told he must return home before the Test series starts because his back problems will prevent him from bowling and fulfilling his role as an all-rounder. Misses next seventeen Tests.

SEPTEMBER 2001 – Poor fitness and form leads to Flintoff being told to sort himself out. Calls Duncan Fletcher and asks to attend Rod Marsh's National Academy in Adelaide at his own expense.

NOVEMBER 2001 – Called up from National Academy, Adelaide, to England's tour of India as cover for injured Craig White. Opens the bowling in an England Test for the first time with Matthew Hoggard in Second Test at Ahmedabad.

DECEMBER 2001 – Reduced to tears by failures with the bat (26 runs in five Test innings) at Bangalore but takes 4 wickets for 50 off 28 overs to win Man Of The Match award in Third Test.

FEBRUARY 2002 – In Mumbai, bowls Srinath of India with penultimate ball of Sixth One-Day International to win the game and help England tie the series. Rips off shirt in celebration and earns quiet rebuke but no fine. Records best bowling figures in One-Day International against New Zealand at Auckland, taking 4 for 17.

MARCH 2002 – Makes maiden Test century for England at Christchurch in First Test against New Zealand, adding 281 with Graham Thorpe, a sixth-wicket record for England. Reaches his 100 from 114 balls and is out for 137, comfortably beating his previous highest Test score of 42. Averages over 40 with the bat in the three-Test series.

SEASON 2002 – Appointed vice-captain of Lancashire.

AUGUST 2002 – Out for a duck in both innings of Headingley Test against India, his second Test 'pair' at the Leeds ground.

SEPTEMBER 2002 – Undergoes a delayed double-hernia operation after playing against Sri Lanka and the first three Tests against India. Rehabilitation is slow. Misses another Ashes series against Australia, returning home in mid-December. Misses eight consecutive Tests.

JANUARY 2003 – Rejoins England team, but to play only one VB One-Day International at the end of the tour. Signs bat deal with Woodworm Cricket Company.

MARCH 2003 – Becomes World Cup's most economical bowler at 2.87 runs per over.

10 MAY 2003 – Overcomes stomach and shoulder problems to score a blistering 111 for Lancashire against Middlesex at Lord's, his first century at the headquarters of cricket. His innings includes four sixes and two changes of bat. Misses two Tests against Sri Lanka with shoulder injury but plays all five against South Africa.

AUGUST 2003 – Hits run-a-ball 142 against South Africa at Lord's, his first Test 100 in England. Highest score by a number seven in a Lord's Test, beating the 137 by England's

Les Ames against New Zealand in 1931. Earns a standing ovation from packed crowd, but England lose the match.

SEPTEMBER 2003 – Named Man Of The Series after setting up England win to square the series with South Africa at the Oval with 95 in 104 balls. Ends season top of Lancashire's County Championship batting averages with 103.80 in five matches and a highest score of 154. Awarded central contract by England and Wales Cricket Board.

NOVEMBER 2003 – Misses Test series against Bangladesh due to groin injury but returns to One-Day team and takes career-best 4 wickets for 14 in first One-Day International and scores 52, not out. In second One-Day International, thumps 70, not out, and equals Ian Botham's England One-Day record of forty-four sixes. Wins third One-Day International with successive sixes in an innings of 52, not out, and passes Ian Botham's England record of sixes in One-Day Internationals. Wins all three Man Of The Match Awards in One-Day series against Bangladesh. Hits ten sixes in the series.

WINTER 2004 – Named one of Five Cricketers of 2003 by *Wisden Cricketers' Almanack*, a prestigious accolade – and the oldest individual award in cricket – first given by the publication in 1889. The five cricketers are picked by the almanack's editor, and the selection is based primarily (but not exclusively) on the players' influence on the previous English season. No player can be chosen more than once.

APRIL 2004 – Takes 5 for 58 – his first 5-for in Tests – against West Indies at Barbados. Bats for five hours and twenty-six minutes to make 102, not out, against West Indies in Antigua in his longest Test innings.

JULY 2004 – Temporarily out of cricket with an ankle injury, but returns to England squad, although unable to bowl. Scores first One-Day 100 against New Zealand at Bristol. Adds another ton two days later against West Indies at Lord's. Smashes West Indies for seven sixes in his 167 – his highest Test score – in Second Test at Edgbaston, Birmingham. Only seven players have hit more sixes in an innings in Test cricket.

AUGUST 2004 – Makes 72 against West Indies in Fourth Test at the Oval, the eighth consecutive Test in which he has passed 50.

SEPTEMBER 2004 – Scores 99 in 93 balls in England's ICC Champions Trophy warm-up match against India. Becomes only the fourth Lancashire player to score a One-Day century for England when he scores 106 off only 121 balls (eleven fours, two sixes) at Bristol. Two days later, becomes the first England player since Marcus Trescothick in 2002 to score centuries in consecutive innings. His innings of 123 contains eight fours and seven sixes and is scored off just 104 balls. Named International One-Day Cricketer Of The Year. Named in World One-Day XI of the Year. Named Player's Player Of The Year.

NOVEMBER 2004 – Rests from England's tour of Zimbabwe, but says he wouldn't have gone anyway.

DECEMBER 2004 – Public vote him into third place behind Olympic Gold medallists Matthew Pinsent and Kelly Holmes in BBC's poll for Sports Personality Of The Year. Contributes 35 to England's first innings and takes vital wickets in the First Test against South Africa to help England to a 7-wicket win, setting a national record of eight consecutive Test victories. Proves an ever-present member of this record-breaking England side, the only Test team to remain undefeated throughout 2004, with eleven victories and two draws.

JANUARY 2005 – Herschelle Gibbs becomes Flintoff's 100th Test wicket in Third Test Match against South Africa at Newlands, Cape Town. Scores his slowest Test 50 from 123 balls in 169 minutes in Fifth Test against South Africa. Hits his fiftieth Test six in this innings, off Ntini. Becomes one of only fifteen players in Test history to have hit fifty sixes. Scores 77 and 14, not out, and takes 6 wickets to help England to a series-clinching draw. Finishes series top of England's bowling averages with 23 wickets, second only to

Hoggard's 26. Bowls more overs in Test series against South Africa than any other England bowler. Flies home to have an operation to sort out his ankle problem.

JULY 2005 – Plays his first Test against Australia at Lord's. Sets a record as the most-capped player (forty-eight Tests) before playing a Test against the Aussies.

AUGUST 2005 – Scores 68 and 73, and takes 7 wickets in the match to inspire England to victory by 2 runs in the Second Test against Australia. His nine sixes in the match beats Ian Botham's record of six sixes in a single Test against Australia. Named Man Of The Match and wins plaudits around the world for his sporting gesture of a consoling handshake for Brett Lee at the end of the match dubbed the greatest Test of all time. Scores 46 and takes 5 wickets in the drawn Third Test at Old Trafford. Sends down 25 overs on the fifth day, the most he has ever bowled in a single day's cricket. Hits 102, his maiden Test 100 against Australia, in the Fourth Test at Trent Bridge. His second innings of 26 guides England towards a famous victory. Named Man Of The Match. Selected for both Test and One-Day World XI squads to play Australia in ICC Super Series.

SEPTEMBER 2005 – Freddie's first innings of 72, and a marathon spell taking 5 wickets for 78 in the Fifth Test at the Oval, propels England towards the draw they needed to regain the Ashes. Freddie is nominated Man Of The Series by Aussie coach John Buchanan after scoring more than 400 runs at over 40 and taking 24 wickets in the series. Freddie is also the recipient of the inaugural Compton-Miller medal for the Man Of The Series chosen from both sides. Named Player Of The Year by the Professional Cricketers Association for the second successive year, the first back-to-back winner since John Lever in 1978–9.

OCTOBER 2005 – Wins Sir Garfield Sobers trophy, the most prestigious individual award in world cricket, when named joint Player Of The Year with South Africa's Jacques Kallis at the ICC awards. Also named in both the One-Day International and Test teams of the year. England win the ICC Spirit Of Cricket Award and ICC President Ehsan Mani cites Freddie's commiseration with Brett Lee at Edgbaston as an iconic moment. Plays for the Rest Of The World in One-Day Internationals against Australia. Takes 7 wickets and hits 35 in Test match between Australia and the Rest Of The World at Sydney. Shane Watson becomes his 150th Test victim.

NOVEMBER 2005 – Takes a career-best match haul of 8 wickets for 156 and hits 45 in First Test against Pakistan. Sir Gary Sobers, the greatest all-rounder ever, is quoted in *The Times* as saying Flintoff is a better all-rounder than Ian Botham.

DECEMBER 2005 – Named BBC Sports Personality Of The Year. He is England's most consistent performer in the One-Day International series against Pakistan. Named at number 72 in *GQ* magazine's list of the 200 most powerful men in Britain.

JANUARY 2006 – Awarded the MBE in New Year's Honours list along with his other Ashes teammates. In a ceremony at Preston Town Hall, Freddie is also given the freedom of Preston, one of only twenty-two people to be honoured in this way in the last hundred years. Begins a benefit year with Lancashire.

FEBRUARY 2006 – Receives MBE from the Queen at Buckingham Palace investiture.

MARCH 2006 – Captains England in a Test for the first time, against India at Nagpur.

Andrew Flintoff Statfile

TEST MATCH CAREER TO DATE: 1998–2006

BATTING										
M	I	N/O	RUNS	HS	AVE	100s	50s	4s	6s	CT
56	90	3	2816	167	32.36	5	18	388	66	37

BOWLING									
M	OVERS	RUNS	WICKETS	BEST	AVE	5WI	S/R	ECON
56	1722	5137	163	5/58	31.51	2	63.41	2.98

ONE-DAY INTERNATIONALS 1998–2006

BATTING

M	I	N/O	RUNS	HS	AVE	100s	50s	4s	6s	CT
98	86	12	2601	123	35.14	3	15	231	83	32

BOWLING

M	OVERS	RUNS	WICKETS	BEST	AVE	5WI	S/R	ECON
98	612	2691	104	4/14	25.87	0	35.30	4.39

TWENTY/20 INTERNATIONALS

BATTING

M	I	N/O	RUNS	HS	AVE	100s	50s	4s	6s	CT
1	1	0	6	6	6	0	0	0	0	1

BOWLING

M	OVERS	RUNS	WICKETS	BEST	AVE	5WI	S/R	ECON
1	3	15	0	–	–	0	–	5

2005: FLINTOFF'S ASHES

BATTING

M	I	N/O	RUNS	HS	AVE	100s	50s	4s	6s	CT
5	10	0	402	102	40.20	1	3	49	11	3

BOWLING

M	OVERS	RUNS	WICKETS	BEST	AVE	5WI	S/R	ECON
5	194	655	24	5/78	27.29	1	48.5	3.37

2004: Flintoff's Golden Year

TESTS BATTING

Innings: 19

Not out: 2

Number of 50s: 7

Number of 100s: 2

Highest score: 167

Runs: 898

Average: 52.82

Catches: 16

BOWLING

Overs: 369.4

Maidens: 78

Runs: 1108

Wickets: 43

Best bowling: 5–58

Average: 25.77

Strike rate per 100 balls: 51.58

Economy rate: 3.00 per over